THREE MEN OF DESTINY

ANDREW JACKSON, SAM HOUSTON AND DAVID CROCKETT

Three Men of Destiny

～ Billy Kennedy ～

Scots-Irish Chronicles [10th Vol.]

AMBASSADOR INTERNATIONAL

THREE MEN OF DESTINY
ANDREW JACKSON, SAM HOUSTON AND DAVID CROCKET
© 2008 Billy Kennedy

The Scots-Irish Chronicles Series (1995-2008)

Cover design & page layout by David Siglin, of A&E Media

ISBN 978-1-932307-96-2
Published by the Ambassador Group

AMBASSADOR INTERNATIONAL
427 WADE HAMPTON BLVD.
GREENVILLE, SC 29609 USA
WWW.EMERALDHOUSE.COM

AMBASSADOR PUBLICATIONS LTD.
PROVIDENCE HOUSE, ARDENLEE STREET,
BELFAST BT6 8QJ, NORTHERN IRELAND
WWW.AMBASSADOR-PRODUCTIONS.COM

The colophon is a trademark of Ambassador International

The author acknowledges the help and support of given to him in the compilation and publication of this book by Dr Samuel Lowry and Timothy Lowry, of Ambassador Productions/Emerald House, Belfast, Northern Ireland and Greenville, South Carolina, United States. Thanks are also extended to Glen Pratt, Amarillo, Texas, for his help.

THIS BOOK IS DEDICATED TO
MY WIFE SALLY, DAUGHTER JULIE AND SON-IN-LAW COLIN.

" I will lift up mine eyes unto the hills, from
whence cometh my help. My help cometh from the
Lord which made heaven and earth".

PSALMS CHAPTER 121, VERSES 1-2:

CONTENTS

ABOUT THE AUTHOR

BILLY KENNEDY

This is the tenth book written by Billy Kennedy in the highly popular series of Scots-Irish Chronicles which details 18th century American frontier settlements by people who left the north of Ireland after emigrating from Scotland during that period.

The books have been eagerly read by tens of thousands of people in both the United Kingdom and the United States, recording as they have the incredible and fascinating story of a proud, dogged and determined people whose contribution to the establishment and development of the great American nation has been outstanding.

Billy Kennedy, who lives in County Armagh, Northern Ireland, has been a leading journalist in Northern Ireland for the past 38 years. He has been an assistant editor, chief leader writer, news editor, political analyst, columnist and churches correspondent with the Belfast News Letter, the main morning newspaper in Northern Ireland and the oldest existing English-written newspaper in the world, founded back in September, 1737 when the movement of the Ulster-Scots (Scots-Irish) to America had begun in earnest.

He is also the editor of The Ulster-Scot newspaper, a popular cultural publication with a large circulation in Northern Ireland and overseas, including the United States.

On his regular visits to the United States over the past 15 years, Billy Kennedy has lectured on the subject of the Scots-Irish diaspora at universities, colleges, historical and genealogical societies and public authorities in cities and towns in the south-eastern and east-coast northern states.

He is a regular broadcaster on news, current affairs and politics with the BBC and other leading media networks in the United Kingdom.

In 2007, he appeared as an historical contributor in the American History Channel documentary, essentially on the remarkable story and achievements of Scots-Irish settlers and their descendants in the south-eastern Appalachian region, titled Hillbilly - The Real Story. He also featured as an author in the 'Word on Word' television series in 1995-1996, presented by John Siegenthaler, from Nashville.

His other main interest is soccer (he has for 35 years been a member of the Management Committee of Northern Ireland's leading Club - Linfield and is currently the Club's Vice-Chairman.) He has written a number of books on that sport.

He also has a great love and passion for American country music, particularly of the bluegrass and Appalachian folk brand and has interviewed many of Nashville's top performers for his newspaper.

He is married with one daughter.

Billy Kennedy can be contacted at 49, Knockview Drive, Tandragee, Craigavon Northern Ireland BT62 2BH. E-mail address - billykennedy@fsmail.net

FOREWORD FROM AMERICA

JOHN RICE IRWIN

We were on our way to the Ulster-American Folk Park in Co. Tyrone in September 2005 when our chaffeur, none other than the prolific author Billy Kennedy, pulled off the main road for a view of the countryside. He proceeded to elaborate to my late and dear wife Elizabeth and I on some points of interest regarding the history and background of that little piece of land called Northern Ireland.

As we walked along, Billy casually mentioned that Ulster was the ancient name of the land before Northern Ireland was officially established in 1921 as a part of the United Kingdom. Two out of every three people there have Scottish and English ancestors. It's a land of lush meadows and low mountains.

Perhaps as a result of my awe and local interest, Billy expanded on the history of this region and its role as the ancestral home of so many great Americans who helped to shape a new country in the 18th and 19th centuries.

Northern Ireland (population 1.7 million) is a tiny place on the northern territory of the Irish island, but its people have had a phenomenal and, we believe, unprecedented positive influence on the development of the United States into the world's most affluent nation.

As we stood there with Billy Kennedy over-viewing the landscape, Billy's enthusiasm waxed more pronounced as I marvelled that so many great, influential and world-renowned Americans emanated from this agrarian little place.

"John Rice, you know that this was the home of President Andrew Jackson's people . . ? Seventeen United States Presidents were of Scots-Irish ancestry from right here in Northern Ireland, and at least six of the 56 signatories of the American Declaration of Independence of July 4, 1776 had family roots here."

The land appeared as rural, rugged, and sparsely population as it must have been when Andrew Jackson's parents Andrew and Elizabeth made the decision to emigrate to America from Co. Antrim in 1765.

The signage at the ancestral Jackson cottage at Boneybefore, near Carrickfergus on the shores of Belfast Lough, indicated that Andrew Jackson's parents, described as poor country folk, lived there and that Andrew had gained renown as a military leader, lawyer, and one of America's strongest and most influential Presidents.

Perhaps no such miniscule piece of this earth has sired so many giants in the development of America as the Province of Ulster, now known as Northern Ireland.

Two questions remained on my mind!

First, what attributes and special characteristics did these people possess that enabled them to become national, even world leaders?

The second perplexing question was: why did so many of this area's sons and daughters leave this beautiful, pastoral and picturesque countryside in the 1700s?

Why would they leave their kith and kin never ever to see them again, and board wooden ships for a risk-laden journey across the Atlantic to a distant and unknown land?

As the first question regarding the characteristics, resolve, innovativeness, integrity and leadership qualities of these people, we won't speculate except to point out that some 75 per cent, it is said, were of Scottish and English ancestry, in the main Non-Conformist and Presbyterian.

They had emigrated mainly from their native Scotland, which lay about 15 to 20 miles across the waters of the Irish Sea and North Channel.

We'll let Billy Kennedy elucidate on these qualities possessed by the Scottish Irish which helped to promulgate them into such heights of leadership and citizenship.

Billy does this principally through the stories, in this book, of three such eminent Scots-Irish men - Andrew Jackson, Sam Houston and David Crockett.

Now, as to the second baffling question? The reason for this rather massive exodus from this quaint and beautiful land of Ulster in the 1700s has always been a wonderment to me. The pastoral countryside of the North of Ireland was rich in history and the low-lying ridges and verdant valleys could hardly have been more inviting.

So why would these people leave a Utopian setting and bid farewell to their families with no expectation of seeing them again? There were political and social expectations, but there were bound to have been more dramatic, pressing and personal reasons to leave such a tranquil land.

The question was poignantly answered a few hours later when we visited the Ulster-American Folk Park near Omagh in Co. Tyrone. On our tour of this most interesting depiction of early life in the north of Ireland, we saw among the several structures on display a small whitewashed cottage of the type so common throughout this land.

We were a bit rushed for time and some members of the party were inclined to pass by this humble dwelling. Billy and I decided to make a cursory inspection of the interior - and the few minutes I spent inside this one abode revealed to me the answer to the question I'd long pondered: why did so many leave their beloved homeland for the uncertainties of the New World?

Inside the dwelling smouldered a sleepy fire fuelled by peat, which was seemingly available in abundance in the area, and the unique aroma permeated the air. Sitting next to the cottage's lone window, near the fireplace, was a lady who immediately impressed me as extremely knowledgeable and familiar with the culture of her people.

I noticed the single bed, one table, two to three chairs, and a few cooking accouterments. Realising that most families had numerous children, I surmised that the furnishings for this dwelling were incomplete.

I asked the lady about the sparse, almost non-existent furnishings. "Where did all the children sleep? Where did they take their meals?"

She pointed to a large shallow, circular basket and explained that the vessel was placed in front of the fireplace at meal times. The potatoes (most often, the only food available) were shovelled from the fireplace into the large woven container, from which all of the family members, seated on the earthen floor, took their meals. Likewise the children slept on the floor, perhaps on pallets with hand-woven bedding.

Suddenly, I realised that no written description could convey the dire deprivation and hopelessness of life for these people. What prospect was there that the young men and women could have a better future?

So it was the bleak and impoverished conditions - exacerbated by the lack of any hope for improvement that propelled them to seek a new life elsewhere. Thus the question became not why these sturdy and ambitions souls left their native homes, but "why wouldn't they have chosen to leave?"

Billy Kennedy, in his 10 books on Scots-Irish descendants and the inestimable contributions they made to the United States of America, has stirred a new interest in and appreciation of these hardy folk.

The conditions they endured shaped their characters, and they, in turn, shaped the history of the United States.

This latest book, Three Men of Destiny, along with the other literary works by Billy Kennedy, not only provide interesting and invaluable information on the Scots-Irish in America, but perhaps, more importantly, it will serve to excite scholars as well as members of the general populace in America to further explore and story this important aspect of their history.

—JOHN RICE IRWIN, Director of the Museum of Appalachia, Norris, Tennessee.

JOHN RICE IRWIN is the founder and director of the Museum of Appalachia at Norris in East Tennessee, 15 miles from the city of Knoxville. Dr Irwin has been a teacher, farmer, businessman, musician and author and his wide range of interests extend to the history, social patterns, music and culture of the south-eastern Appalachian region. His family is of Scots-Irish and Welsh origin. Every October, the annual four-day Fall Homecoming at the Museum of Appalachia attracts tens of thousands of people from every state in the Union and from numerous countries abroad. The Museum is a cherished legacy of East Tennessee folklore and culture.

FOREWORD FROM
NORTHERN IRELAND

IAN ADAMSON

In his landmark study "American's Debt to Ulster", written in the Bicentennial year of the United States of America in 1976, that renowned Ulstermen the Rev Dr Ian R. K. Paisley very aptly summed up the close historical and cultural bonds that have spanned a vast ocean for more than 300 years.

He said: "It is essential that the almost forgotten truths concerning Ulster's enormous and vital role in the founding and establishment of the great American Republic should be re-told both in the United States and in Ulster.

"Every effort to do this must be greatly welcomed. When the story is told the claim that Ulstermen can lift up their heads with justifiable pride will be fully vindicated."

Billy Kennedy was among the first to take up this call by composing his now famous Scots-Irish Chronicles.

For the first of these 'The Scots-Irish in the Hills of Tennessee' in 1995, I was proud to supply the foreword from Northern Ireland.

The cover featured the excellent 'Frontiersman' painting by artist David Wright, of Nashville, Sarah Polk, Rachel Jackson, and those two old adversaries Davy Crockett and Andrew Jackson.

In this latest commentary (his tenth book in the Scots-Irish Chronicles series), Billy tells the story of three complex and interesting men, each of whom was a giant in the history of 19th century America. Jackson and Crockett are joined by Sam Houston, justly described as "the Father of Texas."

Andrew Jackson had been Houston's commanding general in the War of 1812 and Houston became his prodigy in a military and political career which was marked not only by spectacular success, but also by failure and outright despair, caused by his lifelong problem with alcoholism.

Jackson's immense political stature rested unfortunately more on his status as an Indian fighter than on his battle honours at New Orleans in January 1815.

His Indian Removal Act of 1830 resulted in the forced relocation of the Cherokee people from their ancestral homes in Georgia to Oklahoma. The Cherokee tribe were a Christian and agricultural people, who had largely inter-married with the Scotch-Irish (Scots-Irish) in the Tennessee and Carolina regions and were very loyal subjects of the United States.

Yet, as many as 8,000 of them died of starvation, exposure and disease along the infamous 'Trail of Tears' in the winter of 1838-39.

Paradoxically, there was no greater defender of Indian rights and exposer of official corruption than Sam Houston, whose citizenship of the Cherokee nation had been approved by their Council on October 21, 1829.

Davy Crockett, perhaps the most potent symbol of the American frontiersman, was a determined opponent, political and personal, of Andrew Jackson.

It is therefore not surprising that he opposed Jackson on the issue of Indian removal. But like the Indians whom he was unable to save, Davy Crockett became disheartened by Jackson's continual victories and in 1836 left for Texas and martyrdom at The Alamo in March of that year.

As for Sam Houston, Governor of Tennessee and later of Texas, he was forced from office in 1861 for refusing to swear allegiance to the Confederacy and he died in 1863 during the bloody Civil War he had predicted would occur following secession of the Southern states.

How appropriate it is that author Billy Kennedy should remind us again of these three exceptional Scotch-Irish (Ulster-Scots) personalities and their times in the great United States of America so that we can perhaps learn how better to approach the future with greater understanding of the attitudes of other peoples and countries towards us, for the benefit of all mankind.

— COUNCILLOR DR. IAN ADAMSON OBE is a former Lord Mayor of Belfast (1996-97) and member of the Northern Ireland Legislative Assembly.

He is also: Personal, historical and cultural adviser to the former First Minister of Northern Ireland, the Rev Dr Ian R. K. Paisley, MP, MLA.; President of the Ulster-Scots (Ullans) Academy.; Member of the Board of the Ulster-Scots Agency.; Serving Brother of the Order of St John of Jerusalem.; Wisdom Keeper of the Lakota (SIOUX) Nation.; Author of various books on Ulster cultural and historical interests. He was conferred a member of the Order of the British Empire (OBE) by Queen Elizabeth.

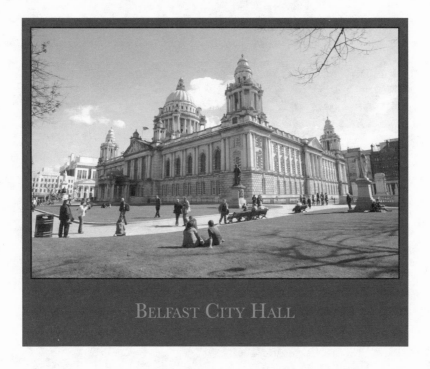

BELFAST CITY HALL

SCOTS-IRISH ARCHETYPES OF THE FIRST UNITED STATES CENTURY

From Andrew Jackson's birth in 1767 during the American colonial era through to David Crockett's death at The Alamo in 1836 and on to Sam Houston's passing in Texas in 1863 as the "War Between the States" raged, these three figures towered above the American historical stage in the dramatic shaping of the United States.

Jackson, Crockett, and Houston not only exemplified the Scots-Irish character, culture, and spirit of their age, but they fashioned what America would become in the first Scots-Irish American century and beyond.

The Scots-Irish epic in America, as witnessed through their lives, would in time become the American epic, not just in their age, but throughout American history down to the present today.

For Andrew Jackson it was from the Waxhaws to the White House; for David Crockett from the Nolichucky River to 'No Surrender' at The Alamo in Texas; for Sam Houston from Timber Ridge in Virginia to the Governorship of Texas.

All three men were of the Scots-Irish (Ulster-Scots) stereotype and they established themselves as archetypes.

1. Their lives were tied into the onwards and upwards movements from Scotland, Ulster and across the larger American continent, taking as the main themes for their lives manifest destiny and mobility and the enhancement of the American frontier.

2. All three had a Scots-Irish background, confirmed through family history, migration and settlement patterns in the American colonies and the United States.

3. They were of humble origins, had little formal education and were largely self-educated; and their families moved west for new opportunities.

    a. Andrew Jackson was orphaned as a child; Sam Hosuton ran away from home as a young man; David Crockett had his grandparents murdered by Indians and he also ran away from home.

    b. All three were products of the American frontier; all three expanded with the frontier and all three helped expand the frontier.

    c. Their occupations fitted the Scots-Irish stereotype of the period – farming, expeditions, hunting, military and politics.

In personality and bravery, they excelled - in bear hunting, alligator wrestling, Indian fighting, duelling, fighting, warfare, the command of men in battle, refusal to surrender, political stances, withstanding scandals, stand-offs.

All were wounded in conflict - Jackson by a British officer's sword and duelist's bullets, Houston at the battles of Horseshoe Bend and San Jacinto or killed - Crockett at The Alamo.

In personality, self-image or reputation, all three portrayed themselves at times or were portrayed by others as rough hewn Westerners.

David Crockett wore buckskin clothes and coonskin cap while in office in Washington and books and plays were written about him.

Andrew Jackson maintained the 'Old Hickory' image as strict and unbending and carried a hickory cane.

Sam Houston had an image as a cool-headed, but sometimes gruff, leader and statesman perhaps on the model of George Washington. He wore on old-fashioned hat at the Battle of San Jacinto in 1836 perhaps to hark back to the Revolutionary era. He also wore his Cherokee costume in Washington D.C.

All were high office-holders in American politics and state affairs including Congressmen, Senators, Governor, President (of the United States and Texas).

On religion, all were Protestants and came from the Presbyterian traditions, although Sam Houston was technically a Roman Catholics for a short time during the colonisation period in Texas (Mexico).

He converted to the Baptist Church under the influence of his last wife Margaret Lea and established Baylor University as a Baptist institution, originally in Independence, Texas.

In relation to the Indians they displayed opposition, pragmatism and accommodation, with paradoxical attitudes toward interaction.

Jackson defeated the Indians in battle and as President pushed theough the policy of removal (Trail of Tears), but he adopted an orphaned Indian boy.

Crockett's grandparents were killed by Indians, he fought against them, reconciled his views towards them, and defended the tribes in Washington during the removal debate sacrificing his political career.

Houston ran away from home and lived with the Cherokees; he warred against them, lived amongst them and he married an Indian squaw, and sought accommodation and peace treaties with them in Texas

Their attitudes may have been a Scots-Irish trait going back to the Borders conflicts in Scotland to accept one's former enemies as a matter of pragmatism when called for.

Andrew Jackson was an avowed enemy of the British during the Revolutionary War and the War of 1812.

Sam Houston courted Britain during the Texas Republic period; he sought recognition and to maintain independent status while feeling out annexation. Again a sign of pragmatism!

In many characteristics and how they chartered their lives, Andrew Jackson, Sam Houston and David Crockett were very similar soul mates.

MAP OF 16TH CENTURY IRELAND

Northern Ireland

Northern Ireland is a region of the United Kingdom, with a population of 1.7million. Its geographical and political boundary takes in six of the nine counties of the ancient province of Ulster.

The majority of the people of Northern Ireland, two-thirds, are committed to maintaining the Union and constitutional link with Britain. A minority seek the unification of Ireland separate from Britain through a political link-up with the Republic of Ireland.

The approximately one million Protestants in Northern Ireland are descendants of Scottish and English settlers who moved from the British mainland to Ulster in the 17th and 18th century Plantation years.

Presbyterians, who formed the bulk of those who emigrated from Ulster to America in the 18th century, belong to the largest Protestant denomination in Northern Ireland. The Church of Ireland (Episcopal) is the second largest.

Belfast (population 500,000) is the capital of Northern Ireland and the six counties are: Antrim, Down, Armagh, Fermanagh, Londonderry and Tyrone.

The main exodus of the Ulster Presbyterians to America came from four of these Northern Ireland counties - Antrim, Down, Londonderry and Tyrone, and from Donegal, one of the three Ulster counties located in the Irish Republic. The others are Cavan and Monaghan.

STATUE OF SAM HOUSTON

AT HIS BIRTHPLACE OF HUNTSVILLE, TEXAS

1

A Common Heritage Which Bonded Jackson, Houston and Crockett

Three gallant men of destiny in 19th century American history had so much in common in family and ancestral ties and in character, mannerisms and political and social outlook as they shaped the fabric of a nation that was in time to emerge as the greatest and most influential in the world.

Andrew Jackson, Sam Houston and David Crockett were a gallant and fearless trio of men who were hewn from the same genealogical and cultural stick that was rooted back across the Atlantic Ocean in lowland Scotland and in the north-east of Ireland (the province of Ulster) a century and more before they were born as first American citizens in what was then the outer ring of the Western frontier.

The families of all three, folk with antecedents in lowland Scotland, had taken the arduous and dangerous passage across the Atlantic from Ulster in the mid-18th century in the daunting quest for freedom and a new life and opportunity in the American colonies.

Indeed, how truly remarkable it was that from this momentous trail-blazing emigration journey, that within a very short period of time, the Jackson, Houston and Crockett names were being carved with enormous pride across this great expanse of land that stretches from sea to shining sea in the United States of America.

The considerable achievements and lasting legacy of these three luminaries are gloriously enshrined in the not so lengthy, but illustrious history of the United States and they are illuminatingly upheld by all those who greatly value and cherish democracy, liberty and independence in this proud and very progressive nation.

Distinctive Scots-Irish family roots identify Andrew Jackson, Sam Houston and David Crockett as members of a dogged and determined race of people who valiantly carried the torch of freedom, independence and their Calvinist religious fervour from the rugged hillsides of Scotland, through the province of Ulster across the Atlantic to the wide open, largely uninhabited spaces of the 'New World'.

Andrew Jackson, born very humbly in a log cabin at the Waxhaw Scots-Irish Presbyterian settlement in the Carolina backcountry on March 15, 1767, was the first common man without a formal education to rise to the American Presidency.

Jackson, the seventh United States President, was a totally different personality from his six Presidential predecessors, who came largely from privileged, aristocratic and positioned Anglo-Saxon backgrounds, and his progression to the White House opened up America as an egalitarian society which placed, as a primacy, opportunity for all of its citizens, no matter their station in life.

The snobbery of the political establishment and the preservation of power in the hands of the few, which had dominated the American Presidency before Andrew Jackson made it to Washington, impacted on Jackson, but, such was his personal commitment to democracy, that he was able to withstand the continual vibes from those who maintained he was educationally and politically unfit for such a high office.

In his time as a state and federal politician and statesman, Andrew Jackson created 'Jacksonian Democracy', a political and social philosophy that was to play such a key role in the shaping of government and decision-making in the United States over the most of two centuries, and, indeed, in establishing what today has become distinctly known as the American psyche.

Indeed, the ascendancy of 'Jacksonian Democracy' is seen by historians and biographers of Andrew Jackson as his greatest triumph.

In his two terms as President (1828-1836), after being unsuccessful in the 1824 election, Andrew Jackson made the United States a genuine democracy, governed by and for the people.

And on his eight-year Presidential watch, he significantly expanded the territorial boundaries of the nation, from the settled regions of the East into the West far beyond the Mississippi River over the Rocky Mountains to the Pacific Ocean, north from the Great Lakes along the full stretch of the Canadian borders and south to Texas, Louisiana, Alabama, Louisiana and Florida and along the Mexican border.

Andrew Jackson was a President who zealously stood first and foremost for the preservation of the Union of the American states and the nation prospered under his firm and inspirational leadership in the eight years he was in Washington.

Sam Houston, also a man with the common touch and the vision and burning ambition to provide a secure and stable future for the America that he loved, was also born into a tightly-knit Scots-Irish Presbyterian community - at Timber Ridge, several miles from Lexington in the Shenandoah Valley of Virginia on March 2, 1793.

The Houstons, like the Jacksons, were solid God-fearing C.o Antrim folk, who, before they emigrated to America, lived within a radius of about 10 miles from each other in Ulster.

While not in any way acquainted or related by family ties, they did share a common heritage, faith and general Protestant Non-Conformist religious and social outlook in life.

Sam Houston, in his role as a Tennessee and Texas politician and statesman in the 1820s, 1830s and 1840s, possessed the fiery drive and enthusiasm that was such a marked characteristic of the typical frontier dweller, who had, over time, succeeded in forging a civilisation out of a bleak and uninviting wilderness.

Houston, believing passionately in the order of manifest destiny, was a highly colourful yet complex man, who, for all of his outstanding achievements, did have some personal failures.

These flaws, perhaps, may have blocked his way to the highest office in the land - the Presidency - and they gave opponents the opportunity and excuse to try and denigrate him.

Sam, bearing the nickname of 'The Raven', had an arrogance and was egotistical, manipulative, even moody, but the Houston drive and dynamism was insatiable and rewarding, not just for himself but for those who gave heed to his inspiring leadership.

His oratory and grasp of the complex political and social issues at hand gave him the edge over opponents and, inevitably, he did have a significant number of enemies in high places.

This was particularly evident when, within a decade, he skilfully charted independence and Republic-status for Texas from Mexican control in the early 1840s to his ultimate satisfaction of it becoming an integral state of the American Union.

It took considerable political skills and acumen to achieve this, but Sam Houston was a quite unique personality in the United States of the early 19th century, a man who dynamically led from the front.

Indeed, Sam Houston's initiative and highly engaging role as Governor at separate times of two pioneering frontier states - Tennessee and Texas - marked him down as one of the really outstanding American politicians, statesmen and libertarians of the 19th century.

His conquests in Mexico and Texas excited citizens in the embryonic and expanding nation and with his patron, mentor and idol - Andrew Jackson - they made a formidable pair, and together they created a political movement that became identified as 'Jacksonian Democracy' which caught the mood in America at that time.

The parallels and similarities in their lives and careers were indeed remarkable. Neither had a formal education, a sensitive subject with both men, and, while both became lawyers, their practices were limited, so preoccupied were they with the military and political matters that were to be at the cornerstone of their careers.

They engaged as major generals in the Tennessee militia, and from the state Congress they progressed to Washington as United States Senators.

And while Andrew Jackson helped draw up the state constitution in Tennessee in the 1790s, Sam Houston, a generation and more later in the 1830s, was just as active in framing the state constitution in Texas, after a parting of the ways from Mexican influences.

They were also active members of the Masonic Order, helping to organise Tennessee's first lodge.

Andrew Jackson, for more than 30 years until his death in 1845, was a father figure for Sam Houston, who regularly sought advice help and counsel from the President and was a frequent visitor to Jackson's home at The Hermitage in Nashville.

In the battles they had a key role in (New Orleans for Jackson - January 1815) and San Jacinto (for Houston - April, 1836), they were remarkably victorious with the smallest losses against much superior forces.

David Crockett, born into an even more humble background than Andrew Jackson or Sam Houston - at Limestone township in north-east Tennessee on August 17, 1786, was a man of real adventure in the wild and rugged countryside of the outer Western frontier.

Crockett did fulfil political ambitions to reach Washington as an elected politician (a Congessman) from "the cane" and he did get some deserved recognition in the capital, even to the point of being promoted by the Whigs as a possible Presidential candidate for the election of 1836.

However, much to David's disappointment, this political ambition lost impetus when he was defeated in a Congress election in 1835.

Crockett's national fame and acclaim came more from his fearless role as a very courageous frontiersman, hunter and militia soldier, who was forever restless and keen to keep always on the move.

David Crockett was much more comfortable living out his life in the company of his own people - in the hilly backwoods of Tennessee. He was most at ease in that environment, a man who never shirked, ever a challenge.

Tragically, it was his willingness to take on daring, and almost impossible military assignments, which tragically resulted in him losing his life with many compatriots of similar outlook and gallantry in what emerged as a totally impossible situation at The Alamo at San Antonio, Texas in March, 1836, at the age of only 49.

Whilst Andrew Jackson, Sam Houston and David Crockett never made it to either Scotland or the north of Ireland during their lifetimes, they were very conscious of their family roots across the Atlantic land and the tribe of people they were born into.

Back in the Ulster homeland, Andrew Jackson was described by admirers as "the great Irish President of the United States" - both in his lifetime, and posthumously.

Jackson, Houston and Crockett had an awful lot in common - in every way, they were three stout men of destiny!

ANDREW JACKSON
by ralph earl

2

THE ULSTER CONNECTION:
ANDREW JACKSON

Andrew Jackson's parents, Andrew and Elizabeth Jackson, were both of lowland Scottish Presbyterian stock who had settled in the north of Ireland (Ulster) during the Plantation initiated by King James 1 from 1606, continuing through the 17th century and into the 18th century.

The Jackson clan had moved from Wigtonshire in south-west Scotland (the Galloway region) across the short North Channel sea journey to Co. Antrim about 1639 and some settled in the area around the busy coastal and ancient borough of Carrickfergus (Crag of Fergus), situated along the coast about 12 miles north from Belfast.

Other branches of the Jackson clan took up residence in counties Londonderry, Down and Armagh and they set the foundations for a family name that today is one of the most commonly held in Northern Ireland.

Renowned Confederate Army soldier in the American Civil War General Thomas Jonathan "Stonewall" Jackson was also of the Jackson clan who moved to Ulster from Scotland in the Plantation years.

His folks lived in Co. Armagh and Co. Londonderry since the Scottish Plantation Ulster before a kinsman - great, grandfather John Jackson - headed to America in the mid-18th century .

Two forebears of Andrew and Elizabeth Jackson - John and Peter Jackson - were made Freemen of Carrickfergus in 1683, just seven years before King William 111 (the Protestant Prince of Orange and newly-crowned British Monarch) arrived at the port with his army on June 14, 1690 to prepare for battle with the Roman Catholic King James II.

It was a battle which the Williamite forces won, and it became the most significant and far-reaching event in Irish history, and indeed in Britain, with a Constitutional Settlement which has been in vogue since. Some historical research points to Andrew Jackson's great-grandfather being a John Jackson, born at Carrickfergus in 1667. He is described as a citizen of some note in the community, figuring in the records sometime as a bailiff of the assize court; he was several times foreman of the court jury and a once member of the town council.

The Jacksons (Andrew's parents) were essentially linen drapers and weavers, productive occupations in the north of Ireland at the time, but, while they would have enjoyed a reasonable self-supporting existence, they were not considered affluent and would not have been significant property owners.

Other Jacksons were small tenant farmers, and fishermen, in both Scotland and Ulster.

Linen weaving had been introduced to Ulster a century before by the French Huguenot Protestants who fled their homeland because of religious persecution and the industry was built up in places like Belfast, Lisburn, Carrickfergus, Larne, Ballymena and Antrim.

Andrew and Elizabeth Jackson lived for a few years of their marriage in the tiny hamlet of Boneybefore, a mile north of Carrickfergus on the Co.. Antrim shores of Belfast Lough.

The first Jackson settlement in Co. Antrim was in the town land of Ball Hill (or Bellahill), close to Ballycarry, a coastal village which lies between Carrickfergus and Larne and a location dominated by the Plantation Bawn landscape, which was built by the Dalway family in the early 17th century.

The Jackson couple (Andrew and Elizabeth), with other members of their family, worshipped in Ballycarry Presbyterian Church, a congregation which was founded in 1642 by the Rev Edward Brice, one of the earliest known Presbyterian clerics ministering in Ireland.

Carrickfergus was the cradle of Irish Presbyterianism and, after the formation of the first Presbytery on June 10, 1642 at the behest of army chaplains of Scottish regiments who were in Ulster at the time, seven Presbyterian congregations were established in that area.

The Church of Scotland (The Kirk) was and still remains the 'Mother Church' for Irish Presbyterianism, today the main Protestant denomination in Northern Ireland.

The Rev Francis Makemie, a Presbyterian minister from Ramelton in Co. Donegal, set up the first Presbytery on American soil at Philadelphia in 1706 and the first Church Synod in 1716, which effectively established Presbyterian Church USA as the mainstream Presbyterian Church in the United States. Makemie emigrated from Ulster in 1683.

For the Jackson clan, the rugged east Antrim coastal region facing the western Scottish coastline was a picturesque homeland, which also became the settling point for thousands of co-religionists from lowland Scotland, lying about 20 miles across the North Channel from Ulster.

The Jacksons and their kin lived through a period of great movement from Ulster to the American colonies and in the 1760-70 decade tens of thousands of people left the main ports of Belfast, Londonderry, Larne and Newry, bound for Philadelphia, New York, New Castle (Delaware) and Charleston.

During that decade, an estimated 21,000 people left Ulster for America in 149 vessels, almost all of them Presbyterians escaping religious persecution and tariffs from the ruling Anglican/Episcopal faction.

In the summer of 1765, Andrew and Elizabeth, with their infant sons Hugh (aged two) and Robert (six months), made the 12-mile journey from their home outside Carrickfergus to the Co. Antrim port of Larne, where they set sail for Charleston, South Carolina.

Larne was a very busy seaport in the mid-18th century and it was also from there that an Andrew Johnson, the grandfather of another American President Andrew Johnson, emigrated to the Carolinas in 1750.

The royal borough of Carrickfergus was part of the extended land estate of Arthur Dobbs, an aristocratic gentleman who settled hundreds of Ulster Presbyterian families in the Carolinas in the mid-18th century.

Dobbs, the Mayor of Carrickfergus and a leading parliamentarian in Ireland, secured large tracts of land in North Carolina and on the Ohio River and served as Governor of North Carolina for a period in the 1750s.

Elizabeth Jackson was of the Hutchinson and Crawford families and there were also connections to the Mecklins and McLins, other Ulster-Scots Presbyterian families who made the trek across the Atlantic. Three Crawford brothers - James, Robert and Joseph, kin to the Jacksons - also left Co. Antrim at that time with their families.

9

James Crawford was married to Jane Hutchinson, a sister of Elizabeth Jackson and a lady whose health greatly deteriorated when she moved to America and became invalid. Four sisters of Elizabeth Hutchinson Jackson had moved to America at the time.

These families would have been encouraged to leave Ulster in the migration initiative launched in Co. Antrim for the Carolinas in the 1740s/1750s by Arthur Dobbs and another British nobleman Henry McCulloch.

Within a short time of their arrival, the Jacksons had acquired 200 acres of poor land at Twelve Mile Creek, a tributary of the Catawba River in the Waxhaw settlement on the North Carolina/South Carolina state line close to Charlotte.

Tragically, Andrew Snr's health deteriorated and he died early in March 1767, leaving a widow, two children and a third child on the way.

Andrew Jackson Snr. had very little financial means, but his close Ulster relatives ensured that he was given an appropriate funeral, together with a traditional Irish wake, before the simple burial in Waxhaw Presbyterian churchyard.

Two weeks later (on March 15), young Andrew was born, a mere 20 months from his family arrived in America, and he and his mother and two brothers went to live with the Crawfords, where Elizabeth Jackson spent 12 years acting as housekeeper and nurse for her ailing sister.

Disputes have arisen as to whether Andrew Jackson was born in North Carolina or in South Carolina, but Andrew repeatedly stated that it was South Carolina. Despite this affirmation, arguments still rage.

In later life, Andrew Jackson recalled how his mother had told him and his brothers of the sufferings of their family in the north of Ireland and the oppression by the High Church nobility there of the labouring poor, many of whom were Presbyterians who had moved to Ulster from lowland Scotland.

When a young man growing up in the Carolinas with a reckless streak, Andrew received an inheritance of £400 from his grandfather Hugh Jackson back in Ireland, but reports confirm he squandered through gambling this money and also acres of his father's farmland at the Waxhaw, which lies 180 miles north of Charleston.

Hugh Jackson, a linen draper, was the father of four sons, the youngest of which was Andrew, the father of a man who was to become an American icon.

The future President was very aware of his Irish roots, but he never ever considered journeying back to the homeland of his parents. During his two terms in the White House, he was sometimes described by admirers on both sides of the Atlantic as "the great Irish President of the United States".

Very few Scots-Irish immigrants, of that period, had neither the will, nor indeed the financial means to venture back across the Atlantic. The prospect of travelling back thousands of miles across the Atlantic did not cross their minds and for most was economically impossible.

In the book 'History of Andrew Jackson' by Augustus C. Buelle, it is recorded that Andrew Jackson, when President in 1833, related to a William Allen, of Ohio, then a young member of United States Congress, and to others assembled at a White House gathering the reasons why his parents emigrated to America in 1765.

The President was reported to have said: "Gentlemen you don't know how near I came to being ineligible to the office I hold. You see, gentlemen, I was born on the 15th of March, 1767. My parents left Ireland in May 1765 and arrived in South Carolina the following July.

"My father had a brother Hugh, who had been a soldier in the Forty-Ninth Regiment of British Infantry. He came to this country with General Braddock, escaped the slaughter of that general's defeat and afterward was with General Wolfe at Quebec.

"During his service in this country - in the year 1756, I believe, four companies of his regiment were sent into Mecklenburg County, North Carolina, in consequence of the threatening attitude of the Cherokees.

"They stayed there for a year and more. Uncle Hugh was a great hunter, but he returned home to Ireland after the end of his term of service, which was in the fall of 1764, and planned to return to raise a colony in the Carolinas."

President Jackson related how his uncle had got married, but could not persuade his wife to emigrate. However, his father Andrew and the three Crawford brothers decided to go with their families, in 1765, on a momentous journey that was in time to resonate in American history.

"You see, gentlemen, that caused me to be born in South Carolina, instead of the Co. Antrim," the President was reported to have said.

Andrew Jackson also said on a visit to Boston on 1833: "I have always been proud of my Irish ancestry and being descended from that noble race. Would to God that Irishmen on the other side of the great water enjoyed the comforts, happiness, contentment and liberty that they enjoy here."

While their Ulster roots, in Presbyterian religion and culture, were never forgotten, Ulster-Scots families like the Jacksons and the Crawfords threw off the mantle of the old country and totally assimilated into American life as home-bred citizens in the cities and towns of the eastern seaboard, south-east Appalachian and western frontier regions.

First and foremost, they considered themselves American citizens with a pride and a stake in their new homeland, even though they were a distinctive breed of people in 18th century America.

Andrew Jackson's wife Rachel was also of a Scots-Irish Presbyterian lineage - the Donelsons, who also moved from Cranmoney (Carnmoney) in Co. Antrim in the early 18th century.

Rachel's father John Donelson was a leading surveyor, patriot soldier and civic leader in the Holston River/Watauga community of East Tennessee (North Carolina) in the 1770s and he was one of the founders of Nashville (Fort Nashborough) in 1780 after an epic land and river expedition from the Holston settlement.

A few feet from the shores of Belfast Lough at Boneybefore, Carrickfergus a plaque is erected which marks the exact locality where the parents of President Andrew Jackson - Andrew and Elizabeth Jackson - lived.

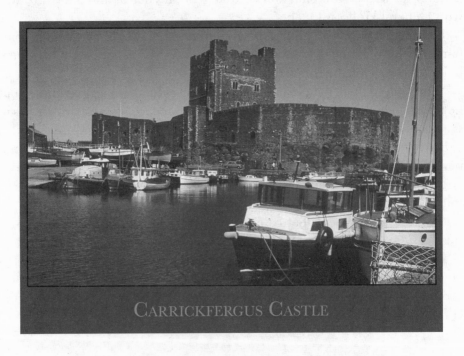

CARRICKFERGUS CASTLE

3

THE ROOTS OF CARRICKFERGUS:
HOME TO THE JACKSONS

Carrickfergus, the Co. Antrim coastal town, where the parents of Andrew Jackson left in 1765, is one of the most ancient settlements in Ireland with an illustrious history that is linked to a line of monarchs.

When Belfast, capital of Northern Ireland, did not exist Carrickfergus was a very important town on the Irish landscape, known at various times as Rock-Fergus, Crag-Fergus and Knock-Fergus.

Carrickfegus is said to have taken its name from Ulster-Scots monarch King Fergus, who lost his life near the site of the town in 510 AD and it developed as a key destination for travellers who moved across the short sea journey from Scotland.

By 1170, the Anglo-Normans were arriving in Ireland, establishing themselves along the coast and it was a young knight from this clan John De Courcy, who felt it expedient to plant a settlement in Carrickfergus, with the town expanding soon after the building of the Castle, Abbey and Church (St Nicholas's Parish) in the period 1177-1204.

Early 13th century British monarch King John lived in the castle for a time and for centuries the town was the chief seat of the English establishment in Ireland.

The Scot Edward Bruce, who was proclaimed King of Ireland in May 1316, was another monarch who used Carrickfergus as a stronghold and with the help of his brother Robert wrested the province of Ulster from English rule.

In the conflicts down the centuries, Carrickfergus was plundered and burned on a number of occasions, but always rebuilt, always around the Castle, in a strategic position overlooking the Co. Down coastline on Belfast Lough.

With the advent of the Protestant Reformation in the early 16th century, religious and political changes swept across Europe and in 1542 Commissioners, authorised by King Henry V111, came across to Carrickfergus to implement the Act of Settlement.

A new Royal Charter for Carrickfergus was obtained in 1569, with consent from Queen Elizabeth 1, and this set forth the loyalty of the town, the suffering of the inhabitants by the rebellions of the Irish and the incursions of the Scots, their gallantry far exceeding any other towns or cities in Ireland and in embracing God's religions and service.

The governance and structures of the town were supported by the Royal Charter, which defined the government and politics of the town and the rights and privileges of the borough.

In 1577, the Earl of Essex, one of Queen Elizabeth's most trusted lieutenants, landed as Captain General and Governor of Ulster, but his adventure there was not a happy one, facing many set-backs from the native Irish, and he resigned his command and retired to Dublin, where he died in 1578.

It was the arrival in Carrickfergus in 1599 of Sir Arthur Chichester which marked a new era in the town and his settlement was effectively the beginning of the English Plantation in Ireland, to be followed a few years later by the Scottish Plantation.

A new Royal Charter for Carrickfergus was issued in 1612 and Arthur Chichester, as Lord Deputy of Ireland, brought stability and prosperity to the town and its Co. Antrim and Co. Down environs.

The logistical and religious difficulties faced by Protestants in Ireland in the early 17th century was a big concern for the British Monarchy and a 10,000-strong army of Scots, under major general Robert Monro landed in Carrickfergus in August 1642 and, with them five Presbyterian chaplains, set about establishing Presbyterianism on Irish soil.

Over the remaining years of the 17th century, the number of Presbyterians grew steadily in Carrickfergus and they were augmented by a colony of fishermen from Ayrshire, who settled in what become known as the 'Scotch Quarter'.

The Presbyterian tradition became dominant in the town and the Jackson clan - forebears of Andrew and Elizabeth and their United States President son Andrew - were among those who moved across from Scotland to settle there.

The most celebrated date in the annals of Carrickfergus was the June 14, 1690, arrival of King William 111, the Protestant Prince of Orange, with his army to prepare for battle with the Jacobite and Roman Catholic monarch James 11.

The battle at the River Boyne near Drogheda on July 1, 1690 confirmed the Protestant succession to the British throne and it unpinned the Act of Settlement for Great Britain and Ireland.

Later, in the mid-1750s a Patriot Club existed in Carrickfergus, which declared in its objectives that it was "ready to defend the King and Constitution" and to "oppose all measures tending to infringe the sacred rights of the people".

Apart from the Andrew Jackson connection, Carrickfergus had other significant links with the American colonies during the 18th century period.

Arthur Dobbs, the man who had the foresight and pivotal role in settling hundreds of Scots-Irish families on the western frontier of North Carolina in the mid-18th century, resided at the family estate Castle Dobbs near Carrickfergus before he headed to America.

Dobbs, born in Girvan, Ayrshire in the west of Scotland, was a leading Irish parliamentarian who took an interest in American political affairs when he was High Sheriff of Co. Antrim and Mayor and Member of Parliament at Westminster for Carrickfergus.

He purchased a part share in 400,000 acres of land in the North Carolina counties of Mecklenburg and Cabarrus in 1745, after the deal was recommended to him by a Co. Antrim associate Matthew Rowan, who was surveyor-general of North Carolina at the time.

Dobbs felt inspired to plant Ulster-Scots Presbyterian families on his new North Carolina lands and he was appointed Governor of North Carolina in January 1753, but it was 18 months before he managed to reach America.

He toured his lands upon arrival in the autumn of 1754, and wrote of 75 families who had settled on frontier land that he owned: "They are a colony from Pennsylvania of what we call Scots-Irish Presbyterians, who, with others in the neighbourhood tracts, had settled together to have a teacher and minister of their opinion and choice."

Dobbs spent more than a decade in America, but his health deteriorated and in 1765 he died, aged 76, and is buried at Brunswick, North Carolina where he had lived.

During the American Revolutionary War, there was another connection to Carrickfergus when revolting patriots began fitting out privateers to prey on the English transports and merchant shipping on this side of the Atlantic.

They ventured into British waters and attacked British shipping and in April 1778, a ship, Ranger, commanded by Scottish-born American naval hero and notorious adventurer John Paul Jones, reached Carrickfergus Bay.

Unrecognised, Ranger hoisted the signal for a pilot and a boat set out from the Scotch Quarter with five fishermen on board, who, when they reached the ship, were taken captive and questioned about a British naval vessel The Drake lying off the Castle.

After several days of stalking The Drake, Jones and his ship's crew prepared for battle and the conflict began when the British vessel bore down on them.

An engagement ensured out in mid-channel of Belfast Lough and it ended with The Drake having two men killed and 25 wounded, one of whom was Lieutenant Dobbs, the second-in-command, and the Ranger three killed and five wounded.

After the fierce one-hour battle, John Paul Jones liberated the fishermen taken prison and sailed for Brest in France before turning to America with The Drake vessel as his celebrated prize.

4

The Ulster Connection:

SAM HOUSTON

Sam Houston, Governor of Tennessee and Texas and a leading American statesman of the 19th century, was also of Lowland Scottish/Co. Antrim Presbyterian roots.

The Houston (Huston) family connection can be traced back to the hilly Ballyboley/Ballynure/Brackbracken area of Co. Antrim that lies halfway between Belfast and Larne beyond the town of Ballyclare.

The Houstons were an enterprising Plantation farming family from lowland Scotland who moved into Ulster in the early 17th century.

In 1729, a famine year for the Scots settlers due to bad weather on the hillsides of Antrim, there was a widow on a small farm of 25 acres in the lowland of Ballybacken called Jane Houston.

She had four sons aged between three and 12 and found that, in spite of assistance from her family and neighbours, she could not pay the rent of the farm to the landlord.

The dire consequence of that in the 18th century Ulster was eviction.

Leases had run out in 1725 and were renewed with an increase. These were years of very low yields from farming and subsequent high prices with the result that scarcely any farmer had surplus to sell and, in many cases, had to use for food the oats and potatoes that should have been stored for seed.

The widow Houston decided that she could not carry on and, in spite of the landlord's agent not pushing for money, she gave up her tenancy.

Under an unwritten law, applying only to the province of Ulster called Tenant Right, she was entitled, on giving up her tenancy, to reimburse for improvements carried out during her tenancy. Her late husband had been an industrious worker.

With whatever money she received from her animals and chattels and the landlord, she set off on foot to the port of Larne, contacting an emigration agent for North America and paying passage money for herself and four sons to New York.

There is no record of her name for that year in the passenger lists from Larne and nothing is known of the time it took to cross the Atlantic or the hardships endured in the voyage.

A few lines by a local weaver poet James Campbell (1756-1818) about another immigrant much later would adequately describe Mrs Houston's feelings as she sailed in the open sea bound for the 'New World'.

"Away to the States frae the port o' Larne
She sailed oot ower the sea,
Like an autumn leaf on the river's drift,
Torn from its native tree".

Houston (Huston) was in the 18th century and still is today a very common name in the East Antrim region between Belfast and Larne, which lies just over 20 miles from the Scottish coastline, and Jane Houston would have been of the same Ulster-Scots clan as the family of Sam Houston.

A lease in the Public Record Office for Northern Ireland from May 1775 records that a John Hume had just over 50 acres of land at Ballyboley and that his neighbours included a Thomas Houston.

The rugged part of Co. Antrim where the Houstons lived was only a few miles from where the forebears of President Andrew Jackson and his father-in-law John Donelson, a leading member of the Watauga community in the north-west Tennessee territory (then part of North Carolina) in the 1770s and founder of Nashville (Fort Nashborough), resided.

From the highest point on Ballyboley Mountain, one can see on a clear day the western coastline of Scotland so the territory was indeed a "hame from hame" for these newly-settled dwellers of Ulster.

John Houston, Sam's grandfather, left the port of Larne for Philadelphia in 1740 with Presbyterian kinsfolk. Within a few years he had reached the Shenandoah Valley of Virginia, where he was instrumental, with others, in setting up the Timber Ridge and Providence Presbyterian churches in that region in the 1750s.

It was an Ulsterman Ephraim McDowell, who led his family and friends from Co. Antrim in 1737 on to the frontier lands they were to call Timber Ridge and, being strong Presbyterians, they continued to worship in the traditional manner they had been taught in their former homelands of Scotland and Ulster.

A call to the Rev John Brown to become the first pastor of Timber Ridge church, situated several miles from, Lexington, was signed by 116 people, with the first signature that of John Houston.

Other signators include the McDowells, Lyles, Davidsons, McClungs Campbells, Paxtons, Thomsons, Mackeys and Alexanders -- all families who had moved a few years earlier to America from Co. Antrim and had married into one another.

Martha Lyle, a daughter of the original emigrant Matthew Lyle, who emigrated with his wife Esther in 1740, married Matthew Houston, son of John Houston, and they and their seven children moved to Blount County in East Tennessee in 1790, settling beside the French Broad River.

This was a trek Sam Houston and his mother and siblings were to take seventeen years later. The Houston clan was to considerably expand in East Tennessee over the decades of the early 19th century

A stone church was erected for the Timber Ridge congregation in 1755-56, sited on an acre of land deeded by Robert Houston, another forebear of Sam, whose link with the area is marked by a memorial stone a few yards from the church.

The cost of building the Timber Ridge church was £150, with Robert Houston, John Berrisford and Daniel Lyle - men of reasonable affluence and standing in this traditional frontier community - raising the bond.

Religion played an important part in the lives of the early Houstons in America, as it did back in Co. Antrim, and indeed it was the Presbyterian Calvinist faith, which had been taken from Scotland a century before, that provided the cornerstone for these hardy frontier families.

Major James Houston, a nephew of John Houston, was an elder in Maryville Presbyterian Church in East Tennessee and six of his daughters married church ministers. He was a state sheriff and a leading militia officer in the Tennessee territory.

Another pastor in the family was the Rev Samuel Houston, a cousin of Sam, and his son the Rev Samuel Rutherford Houston was for many years a missionary to Greece.

The Rev Samuel Houston Snr. was a leading East Tennessee pastor, who graduated from Liberty Hall College in Lexington and ministered at Providence congregation in Washington County. He also soldiered in the Revolutionary War.

Houston was one of the ministers who set up the presbytery of Abingdon and he returned to Virginia to minister in several churches there and establish a classical school. He became a trustee of Liberty and Washington College in Lexington.

The Rev Samuel Doak, who ministered to the Overmountain patriot militia at Sycamore Shoals in north-east Tennessee before they engaged in the Battle of Kings Mountain in the Carolinas on October 7, 1780, was married into the Houston clan. His second wife Margaret was a sister of the Rev Samuel Houston

Doak's parents moved to America from Templepatrick, Co. Antrim in 1739 and he was a highly influential Presbyterian cleric and teacher in East Tennessee, in the late 18th century, establishing Tusculum College outside Greeneville.

Elizabeth Paxton Houston, a stoic, strong-willed woman also of Ulster-Scots stock, was a devout Presbyterian who imparted the Calvinist faith to her nine children.

After her American patriot soldier Sam died, she faithfully guided the family in 1807 from the Shenandoah Valley to a new home at Maryville in the Great Smoky Mountains of East Tennessee.

A John Houston and his wife and six children came from Co. Antrim in 1730 and located at Carlisle township in Pennsylvania. After a few years they were driven out by an Indian uprising and moved to Pequa Valley in Lancaster County.

The Pennsylvania Houstons are thought to be kinsfolk of Sam Houston's family and they had distinguished service in the Revolutionary War, with John's grandson James dying of wounds received at the battle of Paoli.

A brother Dr John Houston, Glasgow-educated, was a surgeon in the George Washington's patriot army and one of the pioneering physicians in York County, Pennsylvania.

· 5 ·

THE ULSTER CONNECTION:
DAVID CROCKETT

The Crocketts - David Crockett's family - arrived in America from the north of Ireland in the early 18th century, having lived in the Tyrone-Donegal counties in the province of Ulster after moving there from Scotland during the 17th century Plantation.

Some historical records claim the family derived from French Protestant Huguenot stock (Crocketagne), who fled France in the 17th century because of religious persecution and they moved over a period of years to Ireland via the north of England and Scotland.

Others, including East Tennessee historian Joseph A. Swann, widely acknowledged as an expert on the Crockett lineage in America, take the considered view that the family were distinctly Scottish by origin, largely concentrated in the Coupar Angus region of central Scotland and at Kirkcudbright near Dumfries in the Galloway region.

It is recorded that several Crocketts bravely defended the walled north-west Ulster city of Londonderry for the Protestant cause in the famous and celebrated Siege of 1688-89 during the Williamite Wars in Ireland.

The north Tyrone hillside town of Castlederg, which lies just a few miles adjacent to Co. Donegal; the nearby Donemana village in north Tyrone, and St Johnston village in Co. Donegal, just a few miles from Londonderry city, were reckoned to be places of residence for the Crockett families after their settlement in Ulster.

Today, in this hilly rural region David Crockett's legendary exploits are revered by the people there, especially by folk bearing the name Crockett.

One of the first Crocketts to reach America during the early years of the 18th century (believed to be 1708) was Joseph Louis Crockett (reportedly born on January 9, 1676 in Co. Donegal), with his wife Sarah Stewart, also from Co. Donegal.

The couple, believed to be David's great-great grandparents, were married at the now disused Abbey Church, Rathmullan, Co. Donegal in 1700; the Stewarts had lived at Ballylawn, Manorcunningham, Co. Donegal, near the shores of Lough Swilly.

A John Crockett is recorded as living in Rathmullan, Co. Donegal in 1650 and a Crockett family also resided at Bogay, where they farmed 300 acres, before moving to Edenmore near Lifford, also in Co. Donegal, today one mile from the Northern Ireland border.

Other Crocketts were settled in the early 18th century at Drumnashear in the Donegal parish of Killea and at nearby Plaster, and the name was also located at Tamlaght O'Crilly and Castledawson areas of Co. Londonderry in the 1740s.

The Crockett connection in Co. Londonderry were members of the Church of Ireland (Episcopal), whilst those in Co. Donegal were mostly of the Presbyterian denomination.

A Rev John Crockett ministered at Castlederg Presbyterian Church from 1832 and this link has given some credence to the local folklore about the Crockett connection in the North Tyrone town.

Government land surveys of 1796 list Crockett families, thus: Co. Donegal - Clonleigh parish (James, John and William Crockett); Killea parish (George Crockett); All Saints parish (Robert, William, Thomas and Archibald Crockett). Co. Londonderry - Tamlaght O'Crilly parish (George Crockett).

Members of these Crockett families inter-married with members of the Gamble, Fulton, Mackey, Hood and Donaghy families of Donegal and Tyrone, local genealogical records confirm.

Indeed, the inter-family link was maintained after emigration to America before and following the American Revolution and Crocketts and Fultons (brothers-in-law George Crockett Jnr. and David Fulton) became involved in merchandising and banking operations in Nashville, Tennessee during the early part of the 19th century.

In 1822, Fulton became treasurer for the Crockett Bank in Nashville and his son David Jnr. studied to be a lawyer with a political associate of Andrew Jackson Felix Grundy and he then served as Jackson's private secretary during the Seminole Indian campaign.

In 1833, President Jackson appointed David Fulton as Governor of Arkansas. The Fultons were a pioneering Ulster family in America, with one of the clan Robert Fulton the man to first apply steam to water navigation. He was born in Lancaster County, Pennsylvania, of Ulster parents who moved around 1730. His father was a founder of the Presbyterian Church at Lancaster.

The Crocketts who headed to America in the early 18th century landed in Pennsylvania, settling for a time in Maryland and New York, before moving down the Great Wagon Road to the Shenandoah Valley of Virginia, and further on to North Carolina, Tennessee and Missouri.

Londonderry was clearly the obvious and nearest port from which the Crocketts emigrated to America, but some historians point to members of the family leaving from Bantry Bay near Cork in the most southerly point in Ireland, hundreds of miles from the Donegal-Tyrone region, where Joseph Crockett and Sarah Stewart were located.

A small settlement of French Huguenot Protestants did settle in the Cork area after arriving from Somerset in the south-west of England in the late 17th century and they pursued viable commercial interests in that city.

Huguenots also settled in Ulster at this time, primarily in the Lagan Valley around Lisburn and Antrim, and they were influential in establishing the highly productive linen industry in the north of Ireland.

However, it seems almost inconceivable in that period of time, when land travel was not the easiest and most accessible, that the Crockett family, located in Co. Donegal, would have trekked from one end of Ireland to the other to board an emigration ship when the main port of Londonderry was virtually on their doorstep, within 10 to 15 miles distance.

The culture, religion and politics of the peoples in the two parts of Ireland then were extremely diverse and moving into unknown, even hostile territory was not advisable. But for a family with Huguenot connections, such a journey could not be entirely ruled out.

David Crockett was a great, grandson of William Crockett (born at New Rochelle, New York in 1709) and it was David's grandfather, also David, who led the family on the very difficult pioneering trek to the outer western frontier.

Tennessee hero David was the fifth son and ninth child of John and Rebekah (Rebecca) Hawkins Crockett and he was born in a one-room cabin in a clearing at Limestone Creek near Greeneville in East Tennessee.

Other branches of the Crockett clan emigrated from Co. Antrim in the 1730s. There are also records of five Crockett brothers from the North Tyrone area - George, James, William, David and Robert emigrating to America with a sister Eliza in the 1796-1811 period. They lived for a while in New York and Baltimore, before heading on to Tennessee.

Edward Mac Lysaght, in his book 'The Surnames of Ireland', relates that the name Crockett is of English origin (believed to be north of England) and the Scottish link is well documented in various publications on the family, as is the Huguenot connection.

The Huguenot tradition in the Crockett genealogy appears in a letter written by David T. Maury, from Essex County, Virginia in 1858 in which he claims to have an old record of the family, brought from France in the early 18th century.

The Crockett family worked for the Maury family, who were Huguenots, and that when they reached Ireland they dropped the name Crocketagne to Crockett.

Other Crocketts who moved from Ulster to America in the 18th century included a Robert Crockett from Co. Antrim who sailed with his wife Margaret in 1730.

Historical records show that their child John Crockett was "born upon sea near Pennsylvania shore."

John's headstone at the Old Waxhaw Presbyterian Church at Lancaster, South Carolina relates: "Lived in America 'til almost fourscore; happy the man who has his sins forgiven, by our Redeemer who now lives in heaven".

Robert Crockett moved from Pennsylvania to Orange or Augusta County, Virginia and he was one the first to purchase land in the Beverley Manor tract at Staunton in the heart of the Shenandoah Valley

His settlement ran to 322 acres and when he died in 1747, aged only 40, this was dispersed among his six sons and one daughter. Some of the family stayed in Virginia, but others moved on to Kentucky, Tennessee and South Carolina.

Today in Northern Ireland, there is a sizeable Crockett clan, with families living mainly in the Co. Londonderry, and North Tyrone areas. The Stewarts, however, are much more numerous, located right across the Province.

BILLY CROCKETT, a member of the clan living at Upperlands, Co. Londonderry in Northern Ireland, has been researching the family history for years and he has visited the Crockett homestead at Limestone in East Tennessee. He observes: "Whenever Crocketts gather in Ireland or America, one notices that they share the same physical characteristics and personality traits so that one instantly realises that they all originally come from the same family."

DAVID CROCKETT

STATUE OF ANDREW JACKSON,
SCULPTED BY CLARK MILLS, IN FRENCH QUARTER OF
NEW ORLEANS, LOUISIANA.

6

JACKSON CHRONOLOGY:
TIME LINE

1636: Jackson clan arrive in the north of Ireland from Wigtonshire in Scotland, settling in Carrickfergus, Co. Antrim and other towns in the province of Ulster.

1683: John and Peter Jackson, forebears of President Andrew Jackson, are made Freemen of Carrickfergus.

1765: Andrew and Elizabeth Jackson, President Jackson's parents, leave their home in Carrickfergus, Co. Antrim for America, sailing from Larne.

1767: Andrew Jackson Snr. dies. Andrew Jackson born at Waxhaw, South/ North Carolina on March 15.

1780: May 29 - attack on the Waxhaw Scots-Irish community by British forces and Andrew Jackson begins service as a boy soldier in the local patriot militia.

1781: Andrew Jackson, then aged 12 , receives facial wound in an affray with a British army officer. Elizabeth Hutchinson Jackson, Andrew's mother, dies after contracting fever on prison ship in Charleston, South Carolina.

1784: Andrew Jackson receives education in Salisbury, North Carolina and teaches for a time at a school.

1787: Andrew Jackson is called to the Bar as an attorney in North Carolina.

1788: Andrew Jackson is appointed public prosecutor for Western North Carolina (later to become Tennessee) and he moves to live in Nashville.

1791: Andrew Jackson marries Rachel Donelson Robards in Nashville.

1795: Elected a delegate to the Tennessee Constitutional Convention.

1796: Elected to the US House of Representatives, but he loses an election for major-general of the Tennessee militia.

1797: Andrew Jackson is first elected to the United States Senate, from the state of Tennessee.

1798: Andrew Jackson resigns US Senate seat, and is elected a judge to the Tennessee Superior Court, serving until 1804.

1802: Andrew Jackson is appointed major-general of Tennessee militia.

1804: Andrew resigns as a judge and he and his wife Rachel move to reside at The Hermitage, Nashville.

1806: Andrew Jackson survives a duel with a Charles Dickinson, who dies in the affray.

1812: The United States war with British forces and the Creek Indians begins with General Andrew Jackson in charge of American forces.

1814: General Jackson is appointed to defend Gulf coast at Florida against British invasion.

1815: General Andrew Jackson leads United States Army in triumph against the British at the Battle of New Orleans on January 8.

1818: After treaties are signed with Indian tribes (Cherokees, Chickasaws and Chocktaws), General Jackson leads United States troops into Florida to defeat the Seminole Indians.

1819: Andrew Jackson transfers Florida from Spanish control to the United States. The Jackson Hermitage home in Nashville becomes a brick house and expansive estate.

1821: General Jackson is appointed Governor of Florida, serves for a period of 11 weeks and then resigns both the Governorship and his United States Army commission.

1822: Andrew Jackson is nominated for the American Presidency by the Tennessee legislature.

1823: Andrew Jackson is re-elected to the United States Senate from the state of Tennessee.

1824: Andrew Jackson runs unsuccessfully for the American Presidency.

1825: Andrew Jackson resigns his US Senate seat to prepare for another Presidential campaign.

1828: Andrew Jackson is elected United States President. Rachel Jackson dies on December 22 and is buried on Christmas Eve at The Hermitage.

1830: President Jackson signs the Indian Removal Bill, leading to the forced movement of native American tribes off their land in the south-east to Oklahoma.

1832: Andrew Jackson is elected for a second term as President.

1836: Andrew Jackson steps down as United States President, and he announces his retirement.

1837: Andrew Jackson retires from public life, retiring to his 1,200-acre plantation (The Hermitage) in Nashville, Tennessee.

1838: President Andrew Jackson formally joins the Presbyterian church.

1845: President Andrew Jackson dies on June 8, aged 79.

BATTLE OF KINGS MOUNTAIN
BY ROBERT WINDSOR WILSON

7

ANDREW JACKSON:

THE EARLY YEARS IN THE CAROLINAS

Andrew Jackson, youngest son of a north of Ireland couple, more than anyone else guided the enormous explosion of the American nation during the first four decades of the 19th century.

His pivotal role in the War of 1812 ensured that the expansive territories on the south-eastern frontier did not fall back into British and Spanish hands.

Jackson's great triumphs as a soldier and general climaxed at the Battle of New Orleans and, of this encounter, he observed with considerable satisfaction: "This morning of January 8, 1815 will be recollected by the British nation and always hailed by every true American."

The General had gone into this battle, defiantly declaring: "I will smash them, so help me God."

In the American mindset, the victory over the British at New Orleans was all down to Andrew Jackson's sterling leadership and he remained a popular hero across the nation for the rest of his life.

Old Hickory - Hero of New Orleans - had restored the confidence of the American nation and he provided reassurance in its ability to maintain its freedom and independence against very heavy odds.

From his days growing up during the Revolutionary War period in the Waxhaw region of the Carolinas - a settlement bearing the name of the

Indians who had once lived there - Andrew Jackson, developed a loathing for British colonial interests on American soil.

His two brothers Hugh and Robert were casualties during the War and his widowed mother Elizabeth, a woman of extraordinary courage and determination, died from cholera fever in 1781 while attending sick nephews on a British prison ship in Charleston harbour in South Carolina.

Andrew, who as a 12-year-old had earlier received a facial wound from the sword of a British soldier during an affray in the Waxhaw, was embittered by these deaths and, alone in the world at the age of 14, he vowed his revenge.

The Waxhaw community was in the direct line of fire during the Revolutionary War and on May 29, 1780 a fierce battle ensued there between a 270-strong British force, commanded by Lieutenant Colonel Banastre Tarleton and 350 men of the 11th Virginia Continentals on the way back to their state, led by Colonel Abraham Buford.

The Continentals lost 113 men and 150 were wounded and they had to be nursed in the Waxhaw Presbyterian Church, with one of the nurses Elizabeth Jackson involved in stenching the men's blood on an improvised straw floor.

Tarleton, who described the Waxhaw community as "a settlement of Irish", listed his casualties as 19 men and 31 horses dead or wounded.

It is claimed that Tarleton ignored the patriots' white flag and pleas for quarter and the attack caused deep and bitter resentment amongst the frontier settler community, with Tarleton, an Liverpool-born English aristocrat who later became an English MP, being despised as "a butcher".

Even today, Carolina folklore characterises him coldly and revengefully as "Bloody Tarleton".

A reported quotation from Andrew Jackson, in later life, recounted: "Tarleton passed thro the Waxhaw settlement to the Cotauba (Catawba) nation passing our dwelling, but all were hid out. Tarleton passed within a few hundred yards of where I and cousin Crawford had concealed ourselves. I could have shot him."

The Buford massacre resulted in many Scots-Irish farmers and their sons queuing up to enrol in militia units that were soon to go into action at the battles of Kings Mountain and Cowpens in the Carolina backcountry. Indeed, the Waxhaw region became a hotbed of American patriotic feeling during the War.

An uncle of the Jacksons, Robert Crawford, was a major in the militia and the teenage boys' eagerness to get involved as patriots in the War was given impetus after witnessing the retreat of General Horatio Gates and his men up the road towards Charlotte after General Lord Cornwallis's victory at the battle of Camden.

The Jackson boys were among 40 local militiamen gathered at Waxhaw Presbyterian Church on April 9, 1781 when a company of British dragoons attacked them with sabres drawn. Eleven of the 40 were captured and the church was burned down.

Andrew, then only 14, tried to escape on horseback with his cousin Lieutenant Thomas Crawford, but they were pursued by the dragoons and captured. In detention, Andrew was ordered to clean the boots of a British officer, but he refused, stating he expected the treatment normally accorded to a prisoner of war.

Insensed by what he saw as a defiant act of insubordination, the British officer then used his sword to strike Andrew's left hand and forehead, leaving a scalp on both which he carried for the rest of his life.

The British then ordered Andrew to lead them to the house of a patriot sympathiser called Thompson, but by taking a roundabout route Thompson was able to escape.

As punishment, Andrew, brother Robert and 20 other militiamen were forced to march 40 miles without food and water, to Camden, where they were confined to prison on a strict diet of bread and water.

For all the professional militarism of his victory and being labelled a hero by his own side back in Britain, Banastre Tarleton lost the propaganda battle in America minds when details emerged that he had allowed "no quarter" even in death for the defeated patriots.

"The demand for quarters was at once found to be in vain; not a man was spared and it was the concurrent testimony of all the survivors that for fifteen minutes after every man was postrate they went over the ground plunging their bayonets into each one that exhibited any signs of life," was one American account of the massacre.

More than 30 years later, just before the Battle of New Orleans, Andrew Jackson told his wife Rachel that "retaliation and vengeance" characterised his attitude to the British and their Spanish and Creek Indian allies.

His personal experiences at Waxhaw during the Revolutionary War shaped Andrew Jackson's character and purpose in life.

He emerged with deep patriot and nationalistic convictions, perceiving himself to be in a struggle for the liberties of his people and not forgetting the price that others had paid to secure them.

These Jacksonian policies became the cornerstone of the Democratic movement which he established in the United States in the early 19th century, a conservative but community-grounded organisation that was the precursor for the Democratic Party of today which in time would pursue policies more to the left of centre.

"I owe to the British a debt of retaliatory vengeance. Should our forces meet, I trust I shall pay the debt - she is in conjunction with Spain arming the hostile Indians to butcher our women and children," said Jackson.

Andrew was born at Waxhaw in the Carolinas on March 15, 1767, a few weeks after the death of his father from the effects of rupturing an internal blood vessel in an injury he is reported to have sustained while felling a log.

Death came suddenly after the injury, Andrew Jackson Snr. was only 29. Jackson Snr. left his wife pregnant with the future President and two tiny sons - Hugh, just four, and Robert two and the family were left virtually destitute.

The remains were carried from the tiny Jackson cabin on a handcart and the simple burial took place in the Waxhaw Presbyterian churchyard at Lancaster County with no stone marking the spot. It was a churchyard which contains the remains of the wider Jackson clan - the Crawfords, McKemeys and the Hutchinsons.

Waxhaw Presbyterian Church was founded by Scotsman the Rev William Richardson, who had earlier established Catholic Presbyterian Church in another part of the Carolinas.

In the journal of C. W. Clerk, itinerant minister in South Carolina 1766-68, the Waxhaw settlement was reported as having a Presbyterian meeting house and pastor, with the Rev William Richardson described as "a good sort of man".

The congregation was described as very large with seldom less than 1,000 assembled for Sunday service.

Andrew Jackson's birth on March 15, 1767 was considered by many historians to have occurred in Lancaster County, South Carolina, but some dispute this, claiming it happened at the adjoining Union county in North Carolina.

In the region, the state lines between North and South Carolina have been blurred and continually in dispute, even to the present day.

Andrew's youthful years were spent in the rough, tough world of the late 18th century Carolina frontier and this prepared him for the rigours of life as a soldier, lawyer, politician and statesman.

Andrew was schooled in York County, South Carolina, under the tuition of a Scots-Irishman Robert McCulloch, and about 1784, he was receiving a higher education in Salisbury, a town 40 miles north of Charlotte on the banks of the Yadkin River. Eventually he moved from being an apprentice saddler to become a teacher, at 17, and a lawyer at 20.

He practised law in Monroe, Anson County, and was a public prosecutor of North Carolina's western district, working in the town of Morganton with a territorial brief that extended from the Mississippi River to the Tennessee territory, land that today encompasses the state of Tennessee.

In 1787 he had been admitted as an attorney to the North Carolina Bar.

Jackson was long and lean and gaunt in physical characteristics, six foot one inch in height and weighing just over 10 stone. He had a very distinctive narrow angular face with auburn hair which had greyed by the time he was President in the 1830s. He had a physical frame which was effectively skin and bone.

He became a charismatic, at times mercurial figure, who, while being combative, quick-tempered and thin-skinned, was also very generous, considerate and loyal to his friends.

Robert V. Remina, a modern Jacksonian scholar, said that to his enemies Jackson could hate with an Old Testament Biblical fury and when in the seat of power, he could be intimidating to those in lesser positions.

James Parton, in his book 'Life of Andrew Jackson', describes the Scots-Irish as a tough, vehement, good-hearted race, who have preserved in full measure the Scottish virtues of honesty, prudence and perseverance, but exhibit the showing traits of the Irish - subdued and diminished.

"They are a plain, simple and pure people, formed to grapple with practical affairs; in dealing with which they often display an impetuosity which is Irish and a persistence which is Scotch. It is in their nature to contend for what they think is right with peculiar earnestness," he said.

Andrew Jackson was a man very much in this mould!

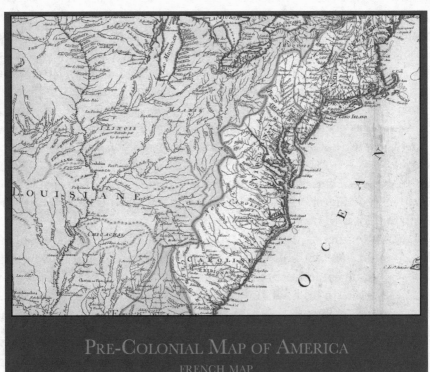

PRE-COLONIAL MAP OF AMERICA

FRENCH MAP

8

ANDREW JACKSON:
MOVEMENT TO THE TENNESSEE TERRITORY

Andrew Jackson moved to the Tennessee territory with others in 1788 trekking along the Wilderness Road over the Allegheny Mountains and arriving in Nashville, which was starting to expand out from its original Fort Nashborough log cabined frontier station, established in 1780.

He opened a law office and met his wife Rachel Donelson, daughter of the Fort Nashborough settlement founder Colonel John Donelson, while staying as a boarder guest in her widowed mother's home.

Rachel had been married before, to Kentuckian Lewis Robards, who started divorce proceedings but dropped these without telling his estranged wife. This meant that Rachel unwittingly committed bigamy when she married Andrew in 1791.

But when Robards later was granted a divorce, the couple remarried and, although they had no children, they had a very happy 37-year marriage. Rachel and, even Andrew, had to endure much slander and insults over the impropriety of their marriage and it became a very controversial, disputed issue during Presidential election time.

Andrew even fought a duel in Kentucky in 1806 with a Charles Dickinson, who spoke harshly of Rachel. Dickinson died from bullet wounds in the pistol shoot-out, while Jackson had rib and chest wounds, but remarkably survived.

It was not the only duel that Jackson had participated in for these combative exchanges were commonplace on the American frontier at the time, but the Dickinson incident was an unfortunate chapter in Jackson's life, and it took several years for him to live it down.

Rachel, even though she was of a family of ten, inherited a substantial amount of property and money from her father's estate and Andrew, until then not a man of great financial means, benefitted and his influence in Nashville expanded considerably in the legal and political sphere.

By 1804, the couple were living at The Hermitage outside Nashville, then a plantation house and farm, and, by 1819, this rustic homestead had made way for a luxury brick house and expansive estate.

They had earlier lived at a homestead in Middle Tennessee called Poplar Grove and at Hunter's Hill.

Jackson's political career began in the Constitutional Convention of Tennessee in the mid-1790s and he was the first Congressman for the state, and later elected a United States Senator. In between, however, his military prowess came to the fore and this established him as a household name across America.

Jackson was appointed major-general of the Tennessee militia in 1802 and for the next 20 years he was seen as essentially a military man.

His first major assignment in the regular army came in 1812 when the War Department in Washington ordered his Tennessee soldiers to Natchez and there dismissed them. Jackson refused to obey orders and he marched his men back to Tennessee, earning for himself in that episode the title of 'Old Hickory'.

"He's as tough as Hickory," his admiring and loyal troops said, and the name stuck with Jackson.

A year on, Jackson engaged his men against the Creek Indians at Talladega, and went on to triumph in other battles against the tribes, in particular at the battle of Horseshoe Bend (March 27, 1814).

The Treaty of Fort Jackson, concluded in 1814, led to the transfer of most of the Creek lands in Alabama and southern Georgia to white settlers.

In May, 1814, Jackson was ordered to defend the Gulf coast against an expected British invasion, and, after leading his troops into Florida and seizing the key port of Pensacola, he marched to New Orleans, where on the morning of January 8, 1815, he routed the British in a battle that has become immortalised in the annals of American history.

Jackson's army consisted of Tennesseans, Kentuckians, Blacks, Indians, and Creoles and, when heavy British artillery fire failed to dislodge them from their location at the dried-up Rodriguez River, British commander General Edward Packenham ordered his 6,500 Crown soldiers to attack head-on.

Within 30 minutes, 2,000 British soldiers were killed or wounded, while only 13 American fatalities were reported. It was the most defining battle between the Americans and the British and in the following month the United States Senate ratified a treaty of peace.

Interestingly, Edward Packenham's British/Anglo-Irish aristocratic family had very large estates at Crumlin in Co. Antrim back in Ulster, less than 25 miles from Boneybefore townland near Carrickfergus where the Jacksons had lived in much more humble surroundings.

Theodore Roosevelt, in his book Naval War of 1812, said that American soldiers deserved great credit for doing so well at the Battle of New Orleans.

He proclaimed: "Greater credit still belongs to Andrew Jackson, who, with his cool head and quick eye, his stout heart and strong hand, stands out in history as the ablest general the United States had produced from the outbreak of the Revolution down to the beginning of the Great Rebellion."

While Jackson may have had his critics over the manner of his victory at New Orleans through the imposition of martial law, suspension of Habeas Corpus and the execution of mutinous militia-men, he won acclaim throughout the nation and, to many, he was a real hero - second only to General George Washington in service to the fledgling American republic.

Old Hickory became an icon of American courage, skill and righteousness. He was hailed as a great military leader, who had raised and trained an effective fighting force that very roundly defeated every enemy he faced.

America's military honour and self-respect was upheld by Andrew Jackson's triumphs, as the nation moved to expand its territorial land borders to the south and to the west.

The Belfast News Letter, a renowned Ulster newspaper founded in September 1737 and which followed very closely the pattern of events in America from the mid-18th century, commented on Andrew Jackson's achievements in an edition of 1829, his first year as President:

"His exploits at New Orleans are fresh in most people's memory. When Jackson entered New Orleans on 23rd January, 1815, after the retreat of the English and the death of Sir Edward Pakenham, he was hailed as the saviour of his country, and a laurel placed on his head . . !" said the News Letter.

An early biographer of Jackson wrote: "Christopher Columbus had sailed; Sir Edward Raleigh and the Puritans had planted; Benjamin Franklin had lived; George Washington fought; Thomas Jefferson written; the population of the country had been quadrupled and its resources increased ten-fold, and the result of all was the people of the United States had arrived at the capacity of honoring Andrew Jackson before all living men."

Andrew Jackson earned 5,000 dollars a year plus expenses as United States Army General, the same salary which he received when Governor of Florida.

Over the next few years, Andrew Jackson successfully negotiated land treaties in Georgia, Alabama, Mississippi, Tennessee and Kentucky, with the Cherokees, Choctaw and Chickasaw Indian tribes.

In 1818, he led troops into Florida, this time to suppress the Seminole Indians and again seized Pensacola and caused an international crisis by ordering the execution of two British subjects suspected of arming the Seminole tribes.

Jackson's hardline stance was vindicated in 1819 when he supervised the transfer of Florida from the Spanish to the United States and, later he served as territorial governor there for three months during the establishment of state government.

His remit extended to captain-general of Cuba, which meant complete military command throughout this highly volatile region.

Jackson resigned his Army commission on June 1, 1821, and in November of that year he and Rachel left Florida for their Hermitage home in Middle Tennessee, where he set about resuming his political career with a vigour which eventually led him to the White House in 1828 for the start of two Presidential terms.

His war service and spell in the swamp heat of Florida took serious toll of Jackson's health. He had two bullets lodged in his body, which regularly formed abscesses and produced coughing spasms leading to massive hemor-rhages. He also contracted dysentery and malaria and developed bronchitis which was to plague him for the rest of his life.

Despite his health strictures, Andrew Jackson managed to soldier on and for the next two decades as a national American politician and statesman he articulated the all-embracing doctrine of Jacksonian democracy.

This argued that it was the obligation of the United States Government to grant no privilege that assists one class over another, to act as honest broker between classes and to protect the weak and defenceless against the abuses of the rich and powerful.

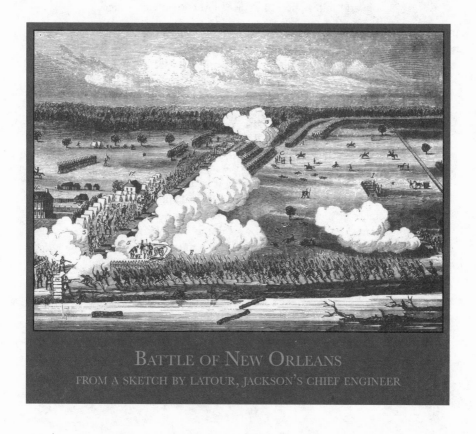

BATTLE OF NEW ORLEANS
FROM A SKETCH BY LATOUR, JACKSON'S CHIEF ENGINEER

"I believe that just laws can make no distinction of privilege between the rich and the poor, and that when men of high standing attempt to trample upon the rights of the weak, they are the fitest objects for example and punishment. In general, the great can protect themselves, but the poor and humble require the arm and shield of the law."
Andrew Jackson, 1821

"Distinctions in society will always exist under every just government. Equality of talents, of education, or of wealth can not be produced by human institutions. In the enjoyment of the gifts of Heaven, and the fruits of superior industry, economy and virtue, every man is equally entitled to protection by law; but when the laws undertake to add to these natural and just advantages artificial distinctions . . . to make the rich richer, and the potent more powerful, the humble members of society - the farmers, mechanics and labourers who hare neither the time nor the means of securing like favors to themselves - have a right to complain of the injustice of their government."
Andrew Jackson, 1832

∙☙ 9 ☙∙

ANDREW JACKSON:

HIS ROLE AS A POLITICIAN AND STATESMAN

Andrew Jackson, as a stump and astute politician, looked beyond the over-arching institutions of American life, linked as they were before to inherited wealth.

To the dismay of Virginia and new England dynasties that had held the Presidency since the country's founding in 1776, Jackson was the first President whose name meant only what he himself could make it mean.

He challenged the power of the Eastern banks, making credit available to less affluent communities in the West, and also resisted threats of secession from the Southern states.

By robustly promoting the West and by holding the United States of America together in one Union, Andrew Jackson set a course for the common man within the nation.

In his policies on the native American tribes, Jackson adopted a paternalistic attitude, dismissing Indian claims of sovereignty over their lands in the south-eastern states. He was heavily criticised for taking this line.

Acting under the authority of the Indian Removal Act of 1830, the Jackson administration forced the various tribes in the south-east to abandon 100 million acres of land and settle in the west, primarily in the Oklahoma territory.

The Cherokee tribes, who inhabited the Tennessee, North Carolina and Georgia region, sued in the American Supreme Court, but they were ultimately forced out of their homelands in what ominously became known as the "Trail of Tears".

It was an event that brought much scorn on the Jackson Presidency and the Washington Administration of the day, but the President took comfort in his belief that removal would not only strengthen the security of white settlers in the southern frontier, who were his own people and constituents, but prevent the inevitable annihilation of the Indians should they remain in the south-east..

After his Presidency, candidates running for office searched in their backgrounds, not for degrees from the universities of Virginia or Harvard or for privilege and patronage from aristocratic backgrounds, but for a frontier log cabin to incorporate in their election manifesto.

Andrew Jackson ran unsuccessfully for President in 1824, losing to President John Quincy Adams in an election that had four candidates - the others were William H. Crawford, of Georgia, and Henry Clay, of Kentucky.

Jackson won the popular vote (152,933 over 115,696 for Adams), with 47,136 for Clay and 46,979 for Crawford. He also won the electoral votes in 11 states; Adams had five; Clay three and Crawford three.

However, because none of four candidates had an overall majority of the electoral votes, the election was directed to the House of Representatives, in accordance with the Twelfth Amendment to the Constitution, and they chose the President from the top three electoral vote winners. In the event, Adams carried 13 states, Jackson seven and Crawford four.

The 1828 Presidential election brought a better outcome for Jackson, defeating John Quincy Adams on the popular vote: 647,292 to 507,730, and on the electoral vote: Jackson 178 to 83 for Adams. Jackson, standing as a Democrat, won the electoral vote in 15 states, and Adams, a National Republican candidate, in nine states.

John C. Calhoun, of South Carolina, whose father Patrick was a Co. Donegal man, was Jackson's Vice-President in his first term. He had also been Vice-President to John Quincy Adams.

In his inaugural Presidential address, Andrew Jackson, not surprising for the national hero of the Battle of New Orleans, struck a military tone, stating: "The bulwark of our defense is the national militia, which in the present state of our intelligence and population, must render us invincible. As long as the government is administered for the good of the people, and is regulated by their will, as long as it secures the rights of person and of as long as it is worth defending, a patriotic militia will cover it with impenetrable aegis."

Tragically, Rachel Jackson died in December 1828, just a few weeks after Andrew was elected for his first four-year term as President.

After just recovering from the shock of the death of their 16-year-old adopted Indian son Lyncoya, Rachel was devastated by the vicious public accusations during the Presidential election campaign of "adultery and bigamy" resulting from her marriage to Jackson before a divorce from her first husband Lewis Robards was sanctioned.

Heartbroken, that she was targeted in this way, Rachel's physical and mental condition rapidly deteriorated and, although Andrew tried frantically to rally her, she died on December 22, 1828 and was buried in the garden of The Hermitage on Christmas Eve.

One of the pall bearers at the funeral was Sam Houston, then Governor of Tennessee and later to become Governor of Texas, and a close political confidante and aide of Andrew Jackson.

For several days, the newly-elected President was inconsolable with grief at the loss of his dear wife and he told his aides: "A loss so great can be compensated by no earthly God".

Andrew had to prepare for the trip to Washington to begin his Presidency, but until the day he died in 1845, Andrew grieved painfully for a loving wife who was so dear to him.

In the 1832 Presidential election, Andrew Jackson won the popular mandate with 687,502 votes over Henry Clay, a Popular Republican, who had 530,189 votes. In the electoral vote he had 219 votes over Clay's 49, winning a majority in 16 states against Clay's six.

John C. Calhoun resigned in December 1832, falling out with Jackson over states' rights, and the new Vice-President was Martin Van Buren, a New Yorker from a Lutheran Dutch background, who succeeded to the Presidency in 1836.

In his inaugural address for his second Presidential term, Andrew Jackson said that without a Union, American independence and liberty would never have been maintained; without Union they can never be maintained.

At the time, there were 24 states in the Union, almost all concentrated east of the Mississippi. Later, during his Presidency, two states were added to the Union - Arkansas and Michigan.

As an American President, Andrew Jackson has consistently been given a high rating by historians, with most placing him in the top six.

The aura surrounding Andrew Jackson's Presidency was also enhanced by his earlier prowess and triumphs as a military general, particularly in the Battle of New Orleans.

He was a President loved, trusted and honoured by ordinary Americans "before all other living men" - as his biographer James Parton pointed out. Yet, several attempts were made on his life, but he survived.

Jackson struck a chord throughout the eight years of his Presidency with populist sentiments such as "the people are sovereign" and "their will is absolute".

His Jacksonian Democracy creed gradually transformed the United States from being a republic to a popular democracy.

·10·

ANDREW JACKSON:
HIS PERSONAL FAITH

For most of his life Andrew Jackson had never been a particularly religious man, but spiritually things changed for him on Sunday July 15, 1838 when he joined the Presbyterian Church.

His mother Elizabeth, who had ambitions of him being a Presbyterian minister, and wife Rachel were both devoted Church members until their deaths and he promised Rachel he would join, but had postponed a decision because he felt a that as a politician a public display of his religion might be regarded as "hypocritical".

Now retired, Jackson consulted the Rev James Smith, who ministered at The Hermitage Presbyterian Church in Nashville, which had been built for Rachel in 1823.

He admitted he felt more identified with the Presbyterian Church than with any other denomination and it was for him an inevitable move.

During the July 15, 1838 service, Jackson rose in his pew to announce that he wanted to join the church, and he further declared belief in its doctrines and resolved to obey the Presbyterian precepts and catechisms.

For the rest of his life, it was said Andrew Jackson conducted himself as a true believer, and his faith was described more uniquely his own than what might be organised with the Presbyterian Church USA, founded by Co. Donegal man the Rev Francis Makemie.

Jackson maintained he could never accept the idea of an "elect" chosen by God, because it offended his democratic soul.

It would have been most uncharacteristic of him to have submitted totally to all the precise teachings of the Church, but he attended services regularly and he read a portion of the Bible each day along with other Biblical commentaries and the hymnbook. He led family and servants in prayers at The Hermitage each night.

Jackson died of chronic tuberculosis on June 8, 1845, aged 78. His health had deteriorated to him having only one functioning lung and his right eye was blind from a cataract. Near the end he could not lie flat in bed, but instead had to be propped up.

His final words were: "Oh, do not cry. Be good children and we shall all meet in heaven."

Two days later, thousands of people gathered on the lawn in front of The Hermitage mansion to pay their last respects and listen to a eulogy as the burial took place alongside his wife Rachel.

Following his death, small silk memorial ribbons imprinted with a likeness of Andrew Jackson were distributed across the nation. They carried images of the Battle of New Orleans and quotations from the old hero. Public memorial ceremonies in cities and towns marked his passing.

In his last will and testament, dated June 7, 1843, Andrew Jackson gave and bequeathed The Hermitage estate to his adopted son Andrew Jackson Jnr.

In the written document, he said: "I bequeath my body to the dust whence it came and my soul to God who gave it, hoping for a happy immortality through the atoning merits of our Lord Jesus Christ, the Saviour of the world.

"My desire is that my body be buried by the side of my dear departed wife, in the garden at The Hermitage, in the vault prepared in the garden, and all my expenses paid by my executor hereafter named."

·11·

The Andrew Jackson legacy

1. Andrew Jackson said on a visit to Boston in 1833: "I have always been proud of my ancestry and being descended from that noble race. Would to God, Sir, that Irishmen on the other side of the great water enjoyed the comforts, happiness, contentment and liberty that they enjoy here."

2. In keeping with the rustic traditions and customs of his age, Andrew Jackson never liked to begin anything of consequence on a Friday, and he avoided, where possible, important business when moving towards the week-end.

3. Martin Van Buren, Andrew Jackson's Democratic successor as President, described Jackson as a man free from conceit.

Another political contemporary Aaron Burr said in 1805: "Andrew Jackson is a man of intelligence and one of those prompt, frank ardent souls whom I love to meet."

4. Many in the aristocratic establishment in the United States never took to "common man" Andrew Jackson as an American President and this view was most prevalent with John Quincy Adams, Jackson's predecessor at the White House.

The urbane, cultured Adams was horrified when Jackson was awarded a degree of Doctor of Law from Harvard University, asking the Harvard President: "Is there no way to prevent this outrage?"

The answer was curt: "As the people have twice decided that this man knows law enough to be their ruler, it is not for Harvard College to maintain that they are mistaken."

Many looked upon Andrew Jackson as "a most uncommon, commoner" - who was rebellious and heroic, one who could stand out against the traditional symbols of privilege.

5. Andrew Jackson was the first American President to ride on a train. In January 1831, during his Presidency, the South Carolina Railroad operated the first American-built locomotive, 'The Best Friend'.

In the same year Cyrus McCormick, a Virginia engineer with direct family roots to Ballygawley, Co. Tyrone in Ulster, invented an agricultural reaping machine.

6. Andrew Jackson's cherished pocket watch is among the many personal items located at his Hermitage home in Nashville.

A black felt hat, made for President Jackson by Washington haberdasher S. W. Handy, is also preserved. Its wide black mourning band honoured the memory of his wife Rachel.

THE ULSTERMAN WAS THERE

Hi! Uncle Sam!
When freedom was denied you,
And Imperial might defied you,
Who was it stood beside you,
At Quebec and Brandywine?
And dared retreats and dangers
Redcoats and Hessian strangers
In the lean, long-rifled Rangers,
And the Pennsylvania Line!
--
Hi! Uncle Sam!
Wherever there was fighting,
Or wrong that needed righting,
An Ulsterman was sighting,
His Kentucky gun with care:
All the road to Yorktown,
From Lexington to Yorktown,
From Valley Forge to Yorktown,
That Ulsterman was there!
--
Hi! Uncle Sam!
Virginia sent her brave men,
The North paraded grave men,
That they might not be slave men,
But ponder this with calm:
The first to face the Tory
And the first to lift Old Glory,
Made your War an Ulster story,
Think it over, Uncle Sam!

— W. F. Marhsall (Rev),
Co. Tyrone

ANDREW JACKSON

DAGUERREOTYPE BY EDWARD ANTHONY

·12·

The Final Hours
of Andrew Jackson

President Andrew Jackson may not have been especially religious during the greater part of his life and until his last years he was not a regular attender of church.

But Jackson was certainly not the heathen some churchmen of the period believed him to be and he never forgot the fundamentals of the Presbyterian faith which his Godly mother Elizabeth taught him as a child growing up in the Waxhaw region of North Carolina.

Jackson's personal attachment to Christianity was experienced by Tennessee Presbyterian cleric the Rev James Gallagher during a pastoral visit to the ageing President at his Hermitage home outside Nashville in 1843.

The Rev Gallagher recalled: "The old hero was very frail and he had the appearance of extreme old age; but he was reposing with calmness and confidence on the promise and covenant of God. He had been a member of the church for several years."

During the conversation which took place, Andrew Jackson turned to the Rev Gallagher and remarked: "There is a beautiful hymn on the subject of the exceeding great and precious promise of God to His people. It was the favourite hymn of my wife Rachel, till the day of her death."

It commences in this way:

"How firm a foundation, ye saints of the Lord,
Is laid for your faith in His excellent word!
What more can he say than to you He has said,
You unto Jesus for refuge have fled?"

Although he took a secular approach to life for most of his life and de-layed formally joining a church until after he had retired to his ancestral Hermitage home in Tennessee, Andrew Jackson enjoyed reading the Bible and he considered himself a practising Christian.

Another favourite book of his was the Oliver Goldsmith classic The Vicar of Wakefield.

Jaclson's wife Rachel was a strongly evangelical Presbyterian, but Andrew did not become an official church member until 1838 after a series of revival services. He said the reason he refused to join the church was that it would be looked upon as political if he did.

Growing up in the Carolinas, Andrew had, of course, learned the basics of religion and he studied the Bible and Catechisms under the tuition of Presbyterian ministers the Dr William Humphries and the Rev James White Stephenson.

His mother had wanted him to become a Presbyterian minister, but it was not to be, as he proceeded to take an interest in law and a civic role, and dab-bled with secular interests that were not compatible with church life. However, he did make a practice of reading Biblical chapters on a daily basis.

At times of crisis and danger during his Presidency, Jackson did publicly express feelings of a dependence on God.

As President, he was deeply conscious of the sharp cultural and religious differences that permeated the American regions and society in the early 19th century.

In his farewell address to the nation, Andrew Jackson said: "In a country so extensive as the United States and, with pursuits so varied, the internal regulations of the various states must frequently differ from one another in important particulars.

"And this difference is unavoidably increased by the varying principles upon which the American colonies were originally planted; principles which had taken root in their social relations before the Revolution, and therefore, of necessity, influencing their policy since they became free and independent states.

"But each state has an unquestionable right to regulate its own international concerns."

Interestingly, Andrew Jackson delivered his last will and testament at The Hermitage, Nashville on June 7, 1843.

After meeting his lawful financial debts to several contemporaries, he bequeathed his home and land at The Hermitage to his adopted son Andrew Jackson Jun., together with other personal belongings.

A few hours after Andrew Jackson died at The Hermitage on June 8, 1845, Sam Houston arrived with his son Sam Jnr. to pay final homage. Sam is said to have taken Sam Jnr. into the home where the body of the dead President lay and said: "Always remember my son that you have looked into the face of Andrew Jackson". Houston, of the same Ulster-Scots vintage as the President, was a long-time admirer and associate of President Jackson! They had so much in common, not least their culture and zest to make it in life.

The Hermitage outside Nashville was more than a home to Andrew Jackson. It was his haven, a peaceful shelter from political tension and turmoil. Here was the centre of his universe - a magnificent mansion amid fertile fields and quiet woodlands. The home Jackson cherished is now an American Natural Historic Landmark that welcomes visitors from all around the world.

Middle Tennessee as it was 150 to 200 years ago is recaptured at The Hermitage of today, with a wonderful museum which contains artefacts and memorabilia belonging to Andrew Jackson and his wife Rachel

RACHEL JACKSON

13

RACHEL (DONELSON) JACKSON: FRONTIERSWOMAN AND PRESIDENT'S WIFE

The extreme harshness of the American frontier during the late 18th century made life very difficult for women young and old as they struggled to keep pace with the enormous challenges encountered by their men-folk in what was a wooded and mountainous wilderness.

Rachel Donelson, who later became the wife of the seventh United States President Andrew Jackson, was only twelve when she and members of her family and Scots-Irish associates embarked on one of the most daunting and perilous journeys in America's early history.

For a girl as young, intelligent and lively as the dark-haired Rachel, the arduous and highly dangerous Holston River voyage to the Cumberland River in Middle Tennessee region obviously left a lasting impression and the harrowing experience was indeed character-building for the numerous personal trials she was to face later in her life.

Rachel (Donelson) Jackson was born in 1767 in Pittsylvania County, Virginia after her parents had moved there from the eastern side of the state where they were married.

John Donelson, Rachel's father was a land-owner and huntsman/surveyor in Virginia and North Carolina who became a leader of the Watauga community which settled during the 1770s on the Holston River of what today is North East Tennessee.

The Wataugans, led by another Scots-Irishman James Robertson, were a hardy, tough breed of people who had the insatiable urge to keep pushing the frontier westwards to new settlements, across the Allegheny Mountains - even against the advice of British land agents who feared the inevitable conflict with the native American tribes.

In that backcountry frontier region, the Indian tribes were the Cherokees and the Chickasaws, some of them hostile to the white settlers and others more disposed to make peace treaties.

John Donelson and James Robertson combined with a North Carolina lawyer and agent Richard Henderson to make an assault on new Tennessee lands on the Cumberland River several hundred miles to the west.

The plans were first prepared in 1777 and Robertson led an exploratory team there over a two-year period, before the decision was taken to move.

A 3,000-acre land grant was negotiated with Richard Henderson and arrangements were made for the movement of these families who were prepared to risk all to start a new life in a far-distant rugged wilderness.

The journey was split with James Robertson assigned to led 200 men and boys with their animals (horses, cows, pigs and sheep) and other belongings on the Kentucky route, along the Wilderness Road and through the Cumberland Gap.

John Donelson, with the welfare of his wife Rachel and young daughter Rachel and his nine other children uppermost in his thoughts, led, with male comrades, the 400 women and children on a flotilla of flat boats from Fort Patrick Henry along the Holston River to the Cumberland River and the new settlement of Fort Nashborough, later to be named Nashville.

River travel, because of the obvious dangers of attack from Indians, was not a favoured mode of communication in that part of the Appalachian frontier, but the Wataugan people felt there no other option.

It was an extremely cold winter - said to be coldest in living memory in North Carolina and the Tennessee territory with the deep snow and frozen rivers making the journey for both parties extremely hazardous, but with dogged determination they persevered and by Christmas week of 1779 Robertson and his men had arrived at their destination.

They were worn out by the rigours of the journey, but began almost immediately to erect log cabins and clear stretches of land for the arrival of John Donelson and the families in the spring. The Cumberland River was frozen over and, incredibly, the animal stock had to be driven across rock solid ice.

The Donelson-piloted party moved in an armada of 40 small flat boats and canoes, moving slowly along the Holston River. The largest boat, Adventure, had 30 families on board, including James Robertson's wife Charlotte and five children and John Donelson's own family, his wife Rachel and the children including young Rachel.

It was an arduous journey into the great unknown for the families; along unchartered waters, over dangerous shoals, rapids and falls; through territory occupied by hostile Indian tribes and in weather conditions that had well below zero temperatures.

After only three miles the voyage was halted; ice and snow and cold had set in and the frozen river made progress impossible. There was no movement until mid-February, and when the boats were eventually cut loose, they were hampered again by the swell of the river due to incessant heavy rain.

Several boats sank and some of the voyagers took ill from smallpox and died. As they passed the Chickamauga Indian settlements the boats came under attack from tribesmen massed on the shore. There were casualties on both sides, with settlers countering the Indian assaults with sniper fire from their long Kentucky rifles.

Most of the boats got through, beyond the danger points, and by the beginning of spring they were at the mouth of the Tennessee River and the high water of the Ohio River.

They faced difficult upstream currents and progress was further hampered, when they had to stop and make camp to replenish dwindling food supplies by hunting buffalo and bear in the adjoining woods.

The last lap of the journey came via the Cumberland River and on Monday April 24 when the party reached French Salt Lick, site of present-day down-town Nashville, there was a hearty welcome from James Robertson and his men who had prepared well for the spring arrival.

When they reached Fort Nashborough in 1780, John Donelson settled his family on fertile bottom land, a few miles from the fort, but this was dangerous territory and with a scarcity of grain and food for the winter, they moved to a more settled area at Harrodsburg, Kentucky in the fall (autumn) of that year.

In 1785, Rachel, in her 18th year, married Lewis Robards, who was from a good family in Mercer County, Kentucky. But it was a relationship which lasted only a few years and Rachel returned to be with her mother, who had moved back to live near Nashville after the murder of her husband in 1786 by persons unknown on the road between Nashville and Kentucky.

The death of John Donelson was a severe blow to his family and it was at her mother's home that Rachel met a young lawyer from North Carolina Andrew Jackson, who was staying as a boarding guest.

The friendship developed and in August, 1791 the pair were married at Natchez, but the marriage to Lewis Robards was never officially wound up which meant Rachel unwittingly committed bigamy when she wed Andrew Jackson.

Robards had filed divorce proceedings to the Virginia legislature, but dropped these without telling Rachel and it was an inconclusive arrangement that was to haunt Mrs Jackson in later years.

By September 1793, Robards did manage to get his divorce, after charging that it was his wife who had deserted him and was living an "adulterous relationship" with another man. The charge was not contested, and Rachel and Andrew went through another marriage ceremony, quietly in Nashville in January, 1794.

Rachel came with a settlement of her late father's estate, which included household articles valued 433.33 dollars and two black slaves. The couple had no children, but they had a very happy 37-year marriage, even though the latter few years were marred by allegations made by political opponents of Andrew over the legality of their marriage, after Rachel's break-up with Lewis Robards.

During the early years of the marriage, Andrew Jackson was a lawyer, circuit judge, land speculator, farmer and businessman. He later moved into politics, was a soldier of national renown especially for his victory over the British at the Battle of New Orleans in 1815 and, eventually, he became President, to serve two terms in Washington from 1828 to 1836.

From a life as a child and teenager in the harsh Tennessee and Kentucky frontier wilderness, Rachel's personal circumstances improved immeasurably and in the several large plantation homes where they lived, her role was more supervisory of the housekeeping and manual duties which were carried out by the servants, among them black slaves.

She hosted regularly gatherings for members of the large family circle and President Jackson's political and business friends, but she fretted much over her husband's long absences from home, due to his exploits as a soldier and politician.

In 1808, they adopted one of twin sons born to her sister-in-law Elizabeth Donelson and, eventually, Andrew Jackson Jnr. was made President Jackson's heir.

Tragically, Rachel Jackson died a few weeks after Andrew was elected for his first four-year term as President. It came soon after the death of another adopted child, 16-year-old Indian son Lyncoya, and the devastated Rachel's condition rapidly deteriorated on learning of the vicious accusations of "bigamy and adultery", made against her during the Presidential campaign of 1828.

Rachel was heartbroken that she should be targeted in this way and, within a few weeks, her physical and mental condition had considerably worsened. Although Andrew tried frantically to revive her, she died on December 22, 1828.

She was buried in the garden of their Hermitage home outside Nashville on Christmas Eve. Among the pall-bearers at the funeral was Sam Houston, then Governor of Tennessee and a close associate of Jackson.

For several days, the incoming President was inconsolable and he told his aides that "a loss so great can be compensated by no earthly gift". He had to prepare for the trip to Washington, to begin his Presidency, but until the day he died in 1845, Andrew painfully grieved for a wife who was so close and dear to him.

Andrew's love for his wife, over three decades of marriage, was evident by the inscription he placed on Rachel's tomb.

It was said he kept his pistols polished and in condition for instant use against anyone who cast a shadow of discredit or doubt on the honour of the woman he loved with "such single-minded, fierce and gentle devotion".

The inscription on Rachel's tombstone read: "Here lies the remains of Mrs Rachel Jackson, wife of President Jackson, who died 22nd December, 1828, aged 61. Her face was fair; her person pleasing, her temper amiable and her heart kind.

"She delighted in relieving the wants of her fellow creatures and cultivated that divine pleasure by the most liberal and unpretending methods; to the poor she was a benefactor; to the rich an example; to the wretched a comforter; to the prosperous an ornament; her piety want hand in hand with her benevolence, and she thanked her creator for being permitted to do good.

"A being so gentle and yet so virtuous, slander might wound, but not dishonour. Even death when he bore her from the arms of her husband, could but transport her to the bosom of her God."

Tennessee historian Oliver Taylor wrote of Andrew Jackson's affection for his wife Rachel: "No political burden ever bore down upon him as did the loss of his companion. His love for her during life and the increasing devotion to her memory are tributes to the strength and amiability of her character."

14

ELIZABETH (HUTCHINSON) JACKSON: DEVOTED MOTHER OF A PRESIDENT

The life and times of Elizabeth (Hutchinson) Jackson, mother of American President Andrew Jackson, were characterised by the natural responsibilities of motherhood mixed with the sense of adventure as an immigrant traveller and frontier settler and experience of real tragedy.

Elizabeth Jackson was an extraordinary woman, of great courage, high purpose and enormous inner strength, a personality that was required to survive on the outer American frontier of the mid-18th century.

She survived her husband Andrew's death and the loss of two sons as a result of action in the Revolutionary War, but, unfortunately, she did not live to see her youngest son Andrew rise to become a successful lawyer, soldier, national statesman and the nation's President.

Andrew and Elizabeth Jackson, both of lowland Scottish Presbyterian families who had settled in Ulster in the 17th century, lived for a few years of their marriage in the tiny Co. Antrim hamlet of Boneybefore, a mile from Carrickfergus on the shores of Belfast Lough.

The Jacksons were linen weavers, a productive occupation in the north of Ireland at the time, but, while they would have enjoyed a reasonable existence, they were not well-off.

Within a short time of their arrival in America the Jacksons had made it to the Carolina Piedmont and settled on a small plot of land at Waxhaw Creek in South Carolina, an area that was also inhabited by the Catawba Indians, considered one of the more friendly of the native American tribes.

Scots-Irish Presbyterians had built a church at the Waxhaw and the Jackson family was assured of a welcome as family connections (the Crawfords and McCamies-McKemeys) and former neighbours from Ulster had settled there.

Branches of the Hutchinson family had also settled at the Waxhaw and at Long Cane (near Abbeville in South Carolina). William Hutchinson was one of the earliest frontier settlers and the family married into the Mecklins or McLins.

Andrew Jackson Snr. had little means to feed his family, although in the less than two years of his life in America he managed to build a log cabin and produce enough crops to see them through. The hard work took its toll and he died suddenly, of unknown causes, in March 1767, just before Elizabeth give birth to Andrew Jnr.

Following a sparse funeral for her husband, Elizabeth moved to the home of her sister Jane Crawford and her husband Robert at nearby Lancaster and, on March 15, the child who was to become President was born, appropriately named Andrew after his just buried father.

Elizabeth had grand ambitions for the fiery, quick-tempered Andrew and, indeed, her other two sons Hugh and Robert. But life was very tough in this part of the American frontier with war clouds looming; the small holding was abandoned and she took up permanent residence with the Crawfords, as a housekeeper and nurse to her ailing sister.

Described as a woman very conversant and industrious, Elizabeth Jackson was said to spin flax beautifully, her heddie yarn spinning was "the best and finest ever seen".

The boy Andrew taught by his mother, could read at five and at eight he was able to write a neat legible hand". In later years, Andrew Jackson recalled long winter evenings when his mother told him and his brothers stirring tales from the Ulster homeland, of their grandfather Hugh Jackson's exploits in battle there and the oppression by the nobility of the labouring poor.

These were tales celebrating courage, pride and independence. Andrew was reported to have received a £400 inheritance from the Hugh Jackson estate back in Ulster.

Young Andrew became a hot-tempered young man, even with the saintly influences of his mother who wanted him to become a Presbyterian minister, and growing up for the first 12 years of his life in a household (the Crawfords) that was not his own he became somewhat impatient, unsettled, and even rebellious.

Indeed, as a youth Andrew had a reputation as being wild, frolicsome, wilful, mischievous and daring. His mother, pre-occupied and wearied with work in the Crawford home, did her best to keep him on the straight and narrow, but without the guiding hand of a father young Andrew was hard to handle.

The Revolutionary War was in progress and the Jackson brothers got caught up in the struggle as the Scots-Irish settler people in the Waxhaw region virtually to a man backed the American patriot movement against British Redcoat forces.

When Elizabeth Jackson and other women of the Waxhaw used their log cabin Presbyterian church (established by the region's first Scots-Irish settlers in 1755) as a hospital for patriot soldiers it was attacked by revengeful Redcoat forces, who, because of the fierce patriot opposition they faced from the local settler community, saw Presbyterian meeting houses as legitimate targets.

Elizabeth's eldest son Hugh, then barely 16, joined the South Carolina militia and, after engaging at the battle of Stone Ferry, he died from the excessive heat of the weather and the fatigues of battle.

It was a second tragedy for Elizabeth and her concerns were increased with other sons Robert and Andrew, a mere boy of 13, also in the militia ranks.

The Jackson boys were at the Battle of Hanging Rock and, on return to the Waxhaw, they were among forty local militiamen gathered at Waxhaw Presbyterian Church on April 9, 1781 when a company of British dragoons attacked them with sabres drawn. Eleven of the forty were captured and the church was burned down by the British.

The Jacksons were arrested by the dragoons while attempting to escape with their cousin Lieutenant Thomas Crawford and, during the initial detention, Andrew was ordered by one of the Redcoat officers to clean his boots. The impetuous teenager bluntly refused, declaring he was a prisoner of war and required to be treated as such.

Incensed at this insubordination, the British officer promptly lifted his sword and aimed it at Andrew's head. Andrew ducked, but he still caught the force of the weapon on his head and fingers and was physically scared for the rest of his life.

With twenty other young patriot prisoners, Robert and Andrew Jackson were taken to Camden, forty miles away, and thrown into jail with 250 other prisoners.

Their prison was an absolute hell hole of a detention centre, with no beds, no medicines and no dressing for their wounds. They contracted smallpox, much to the alarm of their mother who had followed their long trail to Camden, and Elizabeth successfully pleaded with the authorities for the boys' release, as part of the normal war-time exchange between American and British prisoners.

Robert was in very poor shape; he could not stand nor sit on horseback without support. Elizabeth managed to obtain two horses for the arduous journey back to Waxhaw, with the strapped Robert on one mount and herself on the other. The sickly Andrew, barefooted and inadequately clothed for the atrocious weather conditions, walked the arduous and dangerous path home.

Tragically, Robert died within two days. Andrew was in a delirious state and it took all of Elizabeth's devotion and nursing skills, developed from years of looking after her sister Jane Crawford, to pull him through. Indeed, it was months before Andrew fully recovered.

Elizabeth, absolutely committed to a life of care, decided that Andrew was well enough for her to leave home for Charleston, 160 miles away, to nurse American prisoners of war held in prison ships in the harbour.

Her main concern was two nephews, but, poignantly, later in 1781 Elizabeth contracted cholera fever herself while tending to the sick patriot soldiers on the ships and she died after a short illness.

It was a tragic ending for such a courageous woman and, pitifully, her remains were buried in an unmarked grave in the small suburbs of Charleston. The small bundle of Elizabeth's possessions were returned to 14-year-old Andrew, only surviving member of the family. He was distraught, an orphan and sole survivor of his family.

But Andrew remembered words his mother had imparted to him: "Make friends by being honest, keep them by being steadfast; Andy . . . never tell a lie, nor take what is not your own, no sue . . for slander . . settle these cases yourself".

For a time, Andrew Jackson lived at the homes of relatives Thomas Crawford and Joseph White before he was able to decide on his future. He was a victim of the Revolutionary War, losing his mother and two brothers in the conflict.

Their memory and the sad circumstances of their deaths were to live with Andrew Jackson for the rest of his life, right through his military career and two Presidential terms.

He was determined to fulfil the high hopes that his strong-willed mother had for him and his remarkable achievement in reaching the American Presidency was in many ways attributable to the true grit and character which he had inherited from Elizabeth Jackson.

A granite monument at Waxhaw Presbyterian Church erected and looked after by Waxhaw Chapter of the Daughters of the Revolution pays fulsome tribute to Elizabeth Jackson for her extraordinary tenacity and determination in overcoming the many problems which beset the family in this part of the Carolinas during the defining period in the establishment of the American nation.

This is one of the few monuments to Scots-Irish women in the United States, which gives it a very special importance and resonance, and the simple inscription bears lasting testimony to the legacy to one of the outstanding women of the American frontier.

Poignantly, the gravestones of Elizabeth Jackson's two sons Hugh and Robert lie alongside the granite monument.

THE HERMITAGE

PRESENT DAY

15

HOW ANDREW JACKSON IS VIEWED AT THE HERMITAGE TODAY

When his life began no one could have imagined Andrew Jackson as a gentleman farmer, let alone, general, statesman and President. And it all started back when the United States was being born.

This observation is made in the narration of the film script which is shown to the many visitors who come to The Hermitage home of President Jackson at Old Hickory outside Nashville in Tennessee.

"The story of Andrew Jackson begins with the American Revolution. In 1775 American colonies, outraged over the tyrannical rule of Great Britain, turned their anger and their yearning for freedom into armed resistance.

"The Revolution had started and its leaders met on July 4, 1776 to declare independence from the British Crown.

"At the same time, Andrew Jackson was growing up in the tiny South Carolina settlement called The Waxhaws. His parents had left the north of Ireland in 1765 seeking religious freedom, and a better life. In 1780 when Andrew was twelve, the War of Revolution came to The Waxhaws.

"British troops massacred a local detachment of patriot soldiers and pillaged their homes. Young Andrew witnessed the aftermath. Then the war took the lives of his widowed mother and both of his brothers.

"The orphan boy survived, grew up to study law in North Carolina and, as a young prosecuting attorney in 1788, he moved across the Appalachians into the western Carolina district that would later be called Tennessee. His public career began early.

"In those days, the people came to have confidence in him, and he learned the art of leadership. United States' attorney at 23, member of Congress at 29, United States Senator at 30 - accident could not have been responsible for such a career among such a people.

"And over the question of his personal honor in the matter of a horse race, Andrew Jackson fought the one and only duel of his life with a man he believed had grievously wronged him. He mortally wounded his opponent, and walked from the field, concealing the fact that he had been wounded himself.

"When America went to war against Britain again in 1812, General Jackson called his Tennessee militia to active service, though he had no formal military training and had never led his troops in battle! In any assembly of a thousand men, he would have been pointed out above all others as 'a man born to lead'."

The Hermitage narration continues: "Jackson transported his infantry hundreds of miles down river in the dead of winter. But all the fighting was far to the north. The expedition reached Natchez only to be ordered home.

"On the 600-mile march back to Tennessee with his hungry soldiers, one of them, pronounced him 'rough as old Hickory'. It would be Jackson's nickname from then on and he first carried it into battle the following autumn.

"Creek Indians, in league with the British, were attacking the white men encroaching on their lands and Jackson hurled his army against the Creeks in Alabama. In the midst of battle an infant Creek boy, an orphan like himself, was brought to the general. He sent the boy to his wife Rachel, to be adopted."

Then the General imposed a punishing treaty of peace on the Creek nation.

"The next target of the British attack was New Orleans, where Jackson took command as the only American general ever to declare martial law in the United States.

"What followed was one of the great decisive battles in American history. On January 8, 1815, Jackson's Tennessee and Kentucky riflemen routed a British army of 6,000 men inflicting 2,000 casualties. Only 13 American soldiers were killed."

The Battle of New Orleans made Andrew Jackson a national hero. It prevented the British from challenging American expansion into the Gulf

Coast and the south-west. And it convinced Americans they had decisively won a second war of independence.

Jackson said after the battle: "We have laid the foundation of a lasting peace, We have added a country to ours which will become a secure barrier against invasion".

The narration continues with recollections from a visitor setting the scene in August, 1823: "The General came home. The well-wishers who cheered him were the first in a lifelong flood of visitors for the hero who lived at the Hermitage.

"Nashville is agreeably situated on the southern-most bend of the Cumberland River. Steamboats of a large size navigate it for seven months of the year, and smaller boats go about 400 miles higher up. The river is deep and a fine stream.

"About twelve miles above Nashville, in the midst of beautiful and fertile country, occupied by planters, is situated The Hermitage.

"In this delightful house will see the greatest variety of character and company. The manners of the general are so perfectly easy and polished and those of his wife, so replete with benevolence that you are placed at once at ease.

"The Hermitage farm consists of about 1,100 acres of very fertile land, cultivated in cotton and corn, having pastures for a large stock, and high-bred mares and colts, the General being very fond of fine horses.

"Everything at The Hermitage bears the impress of the General's character. All is on a large scale and of a useful and magnanimous caste. He has 110 acres of cotton in the present season, he expects 1,200 pounds an acre of rough cotton.

"He has erected a small brick church in a beautiful grove upon a part of his plantation where the family and neighborhood attend divine services on the Lord's Day. The church was built for Mrs Jackson.

"His devotion to his wife is the gentlest thing in his life. She was a woman of great goodness of heart, benevolence and religious fervor."

As Jackson said: "Heaven will be no heaven for me of she is not there."

In 1831, the narration says, the original Hermitage brick house was enlarged and remodelled.

"Three year later it was gutted by fire and the General had a third house built from the ruins - The Hermitage mansion in final form. It came to be a happy home once more. His adopted son was there and he welcomed Andrew Jnr's bride Sarah as the new mistress at The Hermitage.

"Back in the early 1820s, some of Andrew Jackson's Nashville friends had decided that the general's quiet life at The Hermitage was a waste of great American talent. This was a man, they believed, who should be President.

"They formed a committee and persuaded 'Old Hickory' to run. The Tennessee General Assembly nominated him. He narrowly lost the 1824 Presidential election, then ran again four years later.

"The opposition dug up all the ugly stories they could find about Jackson as a man and a general, and about the circumstances of his wife Rachel's divorce. The Presidential campaign of 1828 was one or the meanest in American history. But when it was over, Andrew Jackson was elected by a landslide.

"There was to be a ball in Nashville celebrating the victory, but shortly after the invitations were sent out, on the day before the event was to take place - Rachel Jackson died suddenly at The Hermitage.

"Her grieving husband went to the White House. John Quincy Adams moved out and Andrew Jackson moved in - the seventh President of the United States.

"Andrew Jackson was the first person to govern with the help of an inner circle of advisors who had more power than the regular cabinet. They were his 'kitchen cabinet' and they reflected his ideas about government service in general."

As Jackson, himself, observed: "The duties of all public offices are so plain and simple that men of intelligence may readily qualify themselves for their performance."

Andrew Jackson was a stubborn, opinionated man who made the Presidency a powerful office, The Hermitage narration acknowledges.

"He believed that control of the nation's money should be in the hands of the elected government not the wealthy directors of an independent bank. So he declared war on the bank of the United States, which represented everything he hated about public power in the hands of the privileged few.

"He persuaded Congress not to renew the Bank's charter, pulled out of all Government deposits, and sealed the Bank's downfall."

As Jackson observed at the time: "If you would preserve your reputation of the state over which you preside, you must take a straight-forward determined course."

The narration continues: "The seventh President was just as determined in matters of foreign policy. When the King of the French failed to pay for damage to American ships on the high seas, Jackson threatened armed retaliation. The King backed down and the United States got its 25 million dollars.

"Some people thought the President was acting like a King. When he promoted the passage of a law forcing the Indians (native Americans) to give up their remaining lands in the south-west, he gave them no choice - stating: 'that you may be preserved as a nation, this may only be done by your consent to remove to a country beyond the Mississippi'."

It is recorded that President Jackson's enemies hated him and rarely saw his good qualities; his friends loved him and reluctantly admitted his failings, and in a sense each was right.

The Hermitage narration recalls how Jackson helped to redirect American expansion toward the South and the South-West.

"When his home state of South Carolina tried to nullify United States laws, the President ended the threat with words that rang in the ears of Americans for years to come: 'can anyone of commonsense believe that a state has a right to secede and destroy this Union. Our Union, it must be preserved'.

"Andrew Jackson made the White House a place of honor for all the Presidents to follow. In the early spring of 1837, after an 18-day journey from Washington by train, boat and carriage, the President came home to The Hermitage."

The President said: "The approbation I have received from the people everywhere on my return home on the close of my official life, has been a course of much gratification to me. I have been met at every point with a hearty welcome and expressions of 'well done thou faithful servant'."

He had been back only four times in eight years, but now he was home to stay. Home where he could visit his wife Rachel's tomb every day at sunset on all the days that were left to him of his long, amazing and sometimes contradictory life.

Andrew Jackson's biographer said of the President: "He was one of the greatest generals, and wholly ignorant of the art of war. He was a democratic autocrat, an urbane savage; an atrocious saint.

"The first of statesman, he never framed a measure. A stickler for discipline, he never hesitated to disobey his superiors.

"Other men excelled him in experience, wisdom and balanced judgment; but the American democrats of the day admired neither of these qualities.

"They honored courage, strength, dedication and directness. Andrew Jackson was the best embodiment of their desires from the beginning of the national government to his own day."

The Hermitage narration concludes: "A President's home is a special place. The Hermitage endures, even when the owner is away. And so do other things: love, honor, our need for a place to call home.

"Tennessee, where Andrew Jackson put down deep roots. And the United States of America which he led into a new age."

* A modest log cabin was the home of Andrew and Rachel Jackson when they first moved to The Hermitage in 1804 and they happily occupied this for 15 years.

In 1819, work began on the construction of a brick mansion, in Federal-style. The two-storey dwelling had four rooms to a floor, two rooms on either side of a central ball.

Ten years after the completion of the mansion, Jackson added a library and dining-room wings and ornamented the façade with a single storey colonnade supported by two columns beneath the second-storey pediment.

The additional structures gave The Hermitage a regal Palladian appearance.

In 1834, the mansion was extensively damaged in a fire, with much of the upper storey destroyed and the first floor also affected.

Renovations began also immediately and in the 1835 transformation, the mansion emerged as a striking example of a fashionable Greek Revival house, which today has become one of the most popular historic locations in the United States, with hundreds of thousands of people visiting the estate every year.

The façade and appearance of The Hermitage remains much as it did when President Andrew Jackson spent his retirement years there in the late 1830s and early 1840s.

The lands, gardens and wooded areas remain an outstanding feature of an estate that was so pivotal and prestigious in the governance of the United States in the first half of the 19th century.

·c·✦16✦·c·

THE JACKS AND THE JACKSONS

One sturdy Ulsterman who, like Andrew Jackson and his kin, was at Charlotte and Waxhaw in the Carolinas with his family at the time was Patrick Jack, who emigrated in 1762 from a farm at Ardstraw in the Sperrin mountain region of Co. Tyrone.

Jack first settled at Chambersburg, Pennsylvania before moving along the Great Wagon Road to Charlotte in North Carolina and he and his five sons were active participants as militiamen in the Revolutionary War.

The Jacks were continually on a wanted list by the British forces, so fervent was their patriotism and desire for American independence.

Indeed, the family home at Charlotte, the area referred to by Lord Charles Cornwallis as the "Hornet's Nest" because of the rapid patriot fervour of the Scots-Irish there, was burned by forces led by Banastre Tarleton in the hunt for Patrick Jack, who hid in a surrounding forest.

Captain Jack was closely associated with the Mecklenburg Declaration in North Carolina on May 20, 1775, which was the forerunner of the Declaration of Independence of July 4, 1776 - a document drawn up and signed mostly by Scots-Irish inhabitants of the region.

Mecklenburg County is very close to Waxhaw, where President Andrew Jackson was born and grew up.

James Jack, a nephew of Patrick, was killed in the Revolutionary War and his 17-year-old son James took his place in the battle lines. James and

Jeremiah Jack are listed as Revolutionary patriots at the Battle of Kings Mountain on October 7, 1780.

The Jacks were a pioneering family in the move west and south during the late 18th century and early part of the 19th century and one illustrious kinsman Colonel William Houston Jack joined Colonel Jim Bowie in leading 140 infantry and cavalry soldiers of the Texas Revolutionary Army against 150 men from the Republic of Mexico Army in the Grass Fight at San Antonio in November, 1835.

The battle, which resulted in a minor victory for the Texans, was a prelude to the siege of The Alamo in March, 1836.

The Grass Fight was so named when the Texans found freshly-cut grass in the mule packs left by the fleeing Mexicans soldiers instead of silver bullion which was rumoured to be on its way to San Antonio.

One consolation for the Texans was that they were able to receive animals and equipment worth 2,000 dollars which they later auctioned

Four of their men were wounded and one deserted and fifteen Mexicans were counted dead on the field, but Jim Bowie reckoned enemy casualties were as high as sixty.

Georgia-born William Houston Jack, who moved to Texas from Alabama in 1832, was a lawyer and a member of the constitutional committee agitating for Texas independence. He was a close associate of Sam Houston and known to Andrew Jackson.

Three American Presidential First Ladies are all reputed to be directly related to Captain James Jack.

Mary Todd, wife of President Abraham Lincoln; Edith Carow, second wife of President Theodore Roosevelt and Helen "Nellie" Herron, wife of President William Howard Taft, have ancestral ties to Captain Jack.

Helen Taft, daughter of Judge John Williamson Herron, of Cincinnati, Ohio, came through this side of the family.

Judge Herron's family are also related to the Rev Francis Herron, minister of First Pittsburgh Presbyterian Church in Pennsylvania from 1811 to 1861. The Rev Herron's father came from Rathfriland in Co. Down.

The Jack family also supplied the only cleric to be named Moderator of the Presbyterian Church of the United States - the Rev Samuel Jack Nicholl, who for for 50 years was pastor of the Fourth Presbyterian Church in St Louis, Missouri.

Another of the Jack family was George Shiras Jnr, who was a distinguished Justice of the Supreme Court of the United States.

THE TWAIN WHOM GOD MADE ONE

They were Twain when they crossed the sea,
And often their folk had warred,
But side by side, on the ramparts wide,
They cheered as the gates were barred.
And they cheered as they passed the King,
To the ford that daunted none,
For field or wall, it was each for all,
When the Lord had made them one.

Thistle and Rose, they twinned them close,
When their fathers cross the sea,
And they dyed them red, the live and the dead,
Where the blue starred-lint grows free;
Where the blue starred-link grows free,
Here in the northern sun,
Till his way was plain, he led the Twain,
Ands he forged them into one.

They were one when they crossed the sea,
To the land of hope and dream,
Salute them now, whom none can cow,
Nor hold in light esteem!
Whose footsteps far in peace in war,
Still sought the setting sun!
With a dauntless word and a long bright sword,
The Twain whom God made One!
— W. F. Marshall (Rev),
Co. Tyrone.

A simple inscription in the vestibule at Greenville Presbyterian Church in the South Carolina Piedmont region sums up the contribution of the Scots-Irish in America: "Sacred to the memory of the Scots-Irish pioneers. From the home land they brought their faith to enrich the South. Their brave hearts and strong arms to subdue the wilderness."

SAM HOUSTON'S SIGNATURE

·∿17∿·

HOUSTON CHRONOLOGY:

TIME LINE

Mid-1600s: The Houston/Huston clan from lowland Scotland settle in the Ulster province in north-east Ireland, locating mainly in east Co. Antrim, close to the part of Larne.

1740: Sam Houston's forebear John Houston emigrates to America from Co. Antrim.

1746: Houston family is involved with other Scots-Irish families in establishing the Timber Ridge Presbyterian Church outside Lexington, Virginia.

1776: Sam Houston's father donates land for the establishment of Liberty Hall Academy at Lexington, which later become the Washington and Lee University.

1783: Sam Houston's father Sam marries Elizabeth Paxton in Timber Ridge Church.

1793: March 2 - Sam Houston born at Timber Ridge, Virginia.

1806: September - Sam Houston Snr. dies.

1807: Houston family led by Elizabeth Paxton Houston moves from Timber Ridge to settle at Maryville in Blount County in the Great Smoky Mountain region of East Tennessee.

1811: Sam Houston graduates as a teacher, aged 18, after being tutored by the Rev Isaac Anderson at new Providence Presbyterian Church academy in Maryville.

1813: March 1 - Sam Houston enlists in the Seventh United States Infantry.

1814: March 26 - Sam Houston soldiers at the Battle of Horseshoe Bend and is seriously injured, but recovers.

1818: Sam is promoted as an Army First Lieutenant.

1820: Sam Houston moves to Nashville to study law and he becomes a district attorney.

1823: Elected to the United States Congress as a Jacksonian Democrat.

1825: Re-elected to the United States Congress.

1827: Elected Governor of Tennessee.

1829: Sam Houston marries Eliza Flora Allen in Murfreesboro, Tennessee on January 22, but the marriage is dissolved after a short period. Sam is re-elected Governor of Tennessee, but resigns shortly afterwards. Sam becomes a citizen of the Cherokee nation.

1831: Sam Houston engages in land treaty talks with Indian tribes. In August his mother dies.

1832: Sam Houston heads to Texas, arriving there on December 2 after crossing the Red River near Clarksville. He reports back to President Andrew Jackson on his opinion of the territory.

1836: January 17 - Sam Houston ordered Jim Bowie to destroy the fortifications at The Alamo in San Antonio. Bowie disagreed, thinking the fortification would be successfully defended. March 2 (Sam Houston's 43rd birthday) - Sam signs the Declaration of Texas and within two days he is immediately appointed commander-in-chief of the Texas revolutionary troops. Siege at The Alamo (an old mission station) ends in defeat for the Americans on March 6. On April 21 the Texas revolutionary troops, under Sam Houston, triumph over the Mexicans at the Battle of San Jacinto, loudly proclaiming the battle cry "Remember The Alamo". Sam Houston becomes President of an independent Texas and takes the oath at Columbia on October 22.

1840: May - Sam Houston marries Margaret Lea, of Marion, Alabama.

1841: Re-elected for a second term as President of Texas.

1842: With the Mexican Army in San Antonio, Sam Houston gives orders to move the public records of the state of Texas from Austin to Houston. This move started the Archives War.

1845: December 29 - Texas is admitted to the Union of the United States.

1846: Sam Houston is elected as a United States Senator from Texas

1854: Converted to Christianity as a Baptist at Independence, Texas

1855: Sam Houston aligns himself politically with the 'No Nothing Party" and campaigns against his former associates in the Democratic Party. He makes an unsuccessful bid to gain a Presidential nomination.

1859: Sam Houston is elected Governor of Texas as an Independent.

1861: Sam Houston refuses to swear allegiance to the Confederacy after Texas' secession from the American Union and resigns as state Governor.

1863: July 26, Sam Houston dies, aged 70. His last words were "Texas, Texas, Margaret . . !" He was buried in a little cemetery near his home in Huntsville.

HISTORY OF THE HOUSTONS (HUSTONS)

The history of the Houston (Huston) clan dates back to the Middle Age feudal years in the Scottish Lowlands, mainly around Renfrewshire.

The name is thought to have originated in a natural way with "Hugh's Town" progressing through various stages to become Hu'ston, Hustoun, Howstoune, and eventually Houstoun, Houston or Huston.

The Houston clan is still very strong in both Scotland and Northern Ireland and in the United States there are an estimated 30,000 people bearing this name.

The variation in spellings of the surname is interesting, differing as it does from family to family. The grandfather of General Sam Houston spelt his name "Huston" in his will. As for pronunciation, the usual form is "Hewston" for either spelling.

SHENANDOAH VALLEY OF VIRGINIA

·18·

SAM HOUSTON:
THE EARLY YEARS IN
VIRGINIA AND TENNESSEE

Sam Houston, who boldly wrested Texas from Mexican control and was the Lone Star State's first President, and later Governor when it was admitted to the Union in 1845, was the grandson of an east Co. Antrim Presbyterian who emigrated to America about 1740.

This teacher-lawyer-soldier-statesmen was a forceful and courageous personality on the American frontier in the early part of the 19th century and, showing a strong streak of independence and all the traditional Scots-Irish characteristics, he blazed a trail from Tennessee to the Tex-Mex border.

The Houston (Huston) family connection can be traced back to the Ballyboley/Ballynure/Brackbracken area that lies halfway between Belfast and Larne. The Houstons were an enterprising Plantation farming family from lowland Scotland who moved into Ulster in the early 17th century.

John Houston left the port of Larne for Philadelphia with his wife, six children and Presbyterian kinsfolk and within a few years he had reached the Shenandoah Valley of Virginia, where he was instrumental in setting up the Timber Ridge and Providence Presbyterian churches at Lexington in Rockbridge County.

Sam Houston (he preferred the name Samuel) was born at Timber Ridge on March 2, 1793, son of Sam and Elizabeth Paxton Houston. His father Sam, a major and later colonel in the militia, was a veteran of the Revolutionary War who soldiered on the frontier until his death in 1806.

Sam's mother was the daughter of John Paxton, another Scots-Irishman from Ulster who was reputed to be the richest and most influential man in Rockbridge County.

"My father was a man of moderate fortune, a man of powerful frame," wrote Sam later, proudly relating how Sam Snr. had served with distinction in General Morgan's Virginia Rifle Brigade under George Washington.

The widowed Elizabeth Paxton Houston moved with her nine children - six sons, including Sam, and three daughters - to Maryville, Blount County in the Great Smoky Mountain region of East Tennessee.

It was a long and dangerous trek in two covered Conestoga wagon through territory that skirted hostile Cherokee Indian settlements, but Elizabeth, then about 50, was a determined woman, and sought a secure future for herself and young family.

Members of the Houston clan had been in the Blount County region since 1795, and, indeed, the first Sheriff of Knoxville and a Secretary of State for Tennessee was a Robert Houston, who had moved from Abbeyville in South Carolina.

Monetary currency at the time and in the expanding region provided a measure of considerable stability and on the trek to Tennessee Elizabeth Houston had in her possession several thousand dollars, a tidy sum of money then which recognised the Houston affluence.

The Houston home in Blount County was on 419 prime acres of land at Baker's Creek, a point close to the Little Tennessee River, which divided the pioneering settlements from the Cherokee Indian lands. The family enrolled at New Providence Presbyterian Church and twice and often three times a week Elizabeth and the children walked the considerable distance over the hills from the Creek to worship.

Elizabeth Houston prospered in her farming interests in Maryville to the extent that she was able to purchase an interest in a general store, a very important business outlet on the American frontier.

At New Providence Church and the adjoining Maryville College, Sam Houston was tutored by highly respected Scots-Irish pastor the Rev Isaac Anderson, who described him as "a young man of remarkably keen and close observation".

Sam was a quick learner and he soon had a firm grasp of the classics. By 18, he had graduated as a teacher and found a position at a small country school which he occupied until he was 20.

In his earlier youth, Sam Houston, an impressive looking man six foot in height, was attracted to the ways of the Indian tribes and he alienated his family when he took up residence at a Cherokee encampment, adopting the Indian dress and costumes and learning the language, considered to be one of the most difficult in the world.

The Indian chief Oolooketa, known as John Jolly, befriended Sam, who was given the title "The Raven", and although he eventually tired of the tribal life and traditions, it was not to be the last time that he aligned himself with the Cherokee people, particularly in the drawing up of important land treaties with the white settlers.

At The French
Trading Post

H. DAVID WRIGHT

·◦19◦·

SAM HOUSTON:

IN THE DIRECT LINE OF FIRE

Soldiering was an ambition for Sam Houston and, in 1813, he enlisted at the age of 20 in the 7th United States Infantry for the war with the Creek Indians and in 1814 he distinguished himself at the Battle of the Horseshoe Bend, where he received three wounds - pierced in the thigh with a barbed arrow and shot twice in the right shoulder.

Sam's bravery under fire and his persistence in vigorously attacking the Creeks, even while he was severely wounded, earned respect from General Andrew Jackson, who was directing the war.

The two men became life-long firm friends and, within a year, Houston was promoted by Jackson from sergeant to second lieutenant, becoming first lieutenant in 1818.

He was in every way a protégé of Andrew Jackson, a man of his times who was to emerge as an American leader of power, vigour and determination in shaping the destiny of the nation towards expansion west and south.

In his role as a major general militia officer, United States Congressman and Governor of both Tennessee and Texas, Sam Houston remained in the confidence and close friendship of President Jackson, and together they developed a strategy that was to expand the territories of the United States from sea to shining sea.

T. R. Fehrenbach, in his comprehensive book Lone Star (A History of Texas and the Texans), described Houston, thus: "He was a great man with the passions of a great man, but in the crucial moments he could exert the iron restraint and discipline of heart and mind all great men must have.

"These qualities, his former fame and the certain knowledge he had the ear of the powerful President of the United States brought Houston to prominence in Texas.

"Sam Houston was an Anglo-Celt of the old tradition. He despised Europe, all its works and its so-called cultured men who willingly seemed to bow to tyrants and aristocracy"

Andrew Jackson used Sam Houston to cultivate better relations with the Cherokees and his knowledge of the Indian language and culture helped him to avert a threatened uprising by tribesmen after the chiefs had surrendered a vast amount of land to the United States Government.

Sam later led a Cherokee delegation to Washington to receive payment for their lands and to legally settle on the boundaries of their allotted reservation.

Houston resigned his United States Army commission, after becoming disillusioned over allegations of complicity in the smuggling of black slaves into the United States. His position was later vindicated in a Washington inquiry and he moved to Nashville, Tennessee, where he studied law and was admitted as an attorney to the Bar.

Sam, in turn, was appointed a district attorney, an adjutant general for the state of Tennessee and major-general in what were to be significant stepping stones to a political career

Sam was elected as a Jacksonian Democrat to the United States Congress in 1823, and re-elected two years later. He became Governor of Tennessee in 1827, and was re-elected in 1829.

When his Presbyterian church marriage in Murfreesboro, Tennessee to 18-year-old Flora Allen faltered after only three months, he resigned the state Governorship in April 1829 and sought refuge with his Cherokee Indian friends, who, by this time, were being prepared for movement off their Tennessee/Carolina lands to Oklahoma in the Andrew Jackson-directed 'Trail of Tears' campaign in the 1830s

Once again, Houston took on the dress, customs and manners of the Cherokees and hunted, fished, attended war councils and lived up to the tribes' habit for intemperance. He was even given an official certificate of adoption into the Cherokee tribe.

During his three years with the Indians, Houston visited Washington several times, on behalf of the tribes in peace and land negotiations. He cohabited with a half-breed Indian woman Tyania Rodgers Gentry. Their association ended when she refused to desert her people on Sam's request.

His own wife, a young woman of position and character in Middle Tennessee, later obtained a divorce for abandonment and she re-married. Houston was a man of varied moods and, when taken to bouts of heavy drinking, he could be a very difficult, prickly individual.

Sam was a man of considerable stature and, by early age, he was over six foot in height, and weighed two hundred and forty pounds, which gave him a mighty presence in any company.

SAM HOUSTON

20

SAM HOUSTON:
ON THE TEXAS TRAIL

Sam Houston in 1832 headed to Texas, then in the middle of a revolution seeking to end Mexican rule. He was warmly welcomed by the American colonists at Nacogdoches and, adopting a very hardline stance on independence for the region, he participated in the convention at San Felipe de Austin (later to become the city of Austin!), which led to the breaking of the Mexican constitutional link.

In a letter to President Andrew Jackson extolling Texas as a region for development and settlement, Sam Houston wrote: "I have travelled near five hundred miles across Texas and am now enabled to judge pretty near correctly of the soil and the resources of the country, and I have no hesitancy in pronouncing it the finest country to its extent upon the globe.

"For the great portion of it is richer and more healthy, in my opinion, than West Tennessee. There can be no doubt that the country east of the Rio Grande of the north would sustain a population of ten million souls. It is probable that I will make Texas my abiding place. In adopting this course, I will never forget the country of my birth."

Sam, always promoting the welfare of the native American Indians, took part in talks with Comanche Indian chiefs on disputed boundary questions in the San Antonio region.

It was while he was in Nacogdoches in 1833 that Sam converted to Roman Catholicism. Texas was at that time under Mexican control and anyone becoming a citizen there had to be a Roman Catholic in faith and practice.

Whether out of expedience or a willingness to dabble in the mysteries of another faith, Houston was baptised as a Roman Catholic and given the name Paul (or Pablo).

However, the enthusiasm for his new religion waned and, within a short period, he was completely at odds with the Papacy and its hierarchal and dominating influence on life in the Texas/Mexico territory, particularly among the indigenous population, who were very poor.

Urging his men to fight Mexico and strongly criticising the Roman Catholic Church's arbitrary power, Sam Houston declared: "Our constitutions have been declared at an end while all that is sacred is menaced by arbitrary power.

"The priesthood and the army are to mete out the measures of our wretchedness. Our only ambition is the attainment of national liberty - the freedom of religious opinion and just laws".

In the spring of 1836, Sam Houston was appointed commander-in-chief of the Texas revolutionary troops and he made the call: "Volunteers from the United States . . . come with a good rifle and come soon. Liberty or death!"

Houston was largely instrumental in the drawing up of the Declaration of Independence for Texas, which was adopted at a convention in the town of Washington without a dissenting voice and formally signed on March 2, 1836.

Eleven of the 58 signers of the Declaration of Texas were natives of Virginia; nine of Tennessee, nine of North Carolina, five of Kentucky, four of South Carolina; four of Georgia, three of Mexico (two from Texas and one from Yucatan), two of Pennsylvania, two of New York and one each of Massachusetts, New Jersey, Ireland, Scotland, England and Canada.

They were a gathering of men from varied political and social backgrounds, all with the passionate belief in their liberty and independence - unquestionably, stout men of destiny.

Sam Houston, studiously laying down a marker, wrote early in 1836: "Independence is the prize for which we battle".

The Texas Declaration, asserting complete independence from Mexico, proclaimed: "The necessity of self-preservation now decrees our eternal political separation. We constitute a free, sovereign and independent republic and are fully invested with all the rights and attributes which belong to independent nations. Conscious of the rectitude of our intentions, we fearlessly and confidently commit the issue to the decision of the supreme Arbiter of the destinies of nations".

The document was signed on Sam Houston's 42nd birthday and on March 4 he was officially sworn in as commander-in-chief of the armies of the Texas Republic.

Houston was called into almost immediate action by the violent events that unfolded from The Alamo in San Antonio that week. There, Mexican President Antonio Lopez de Santa Anna - dubbed by his admirers as "the Napoleon of the Americas" and a 5,000-strong army had laid siege on 189 Texas Rangers and volunteer soldiers from Tennessee, along with a collection of women, children and black slaves.

Tennessee frontiersman David Crockett and another Tennessean Colonel Jim Bowie, two former associates of Sam Houston, were among those besieged at The Alamo, but, ominously, troop reinforcements did not arrive in time and a terrible massacre occurred which stirred the passions of the American settlers in the territory, and when news eventually reached out - the political establishment in Washington.

The Texas Convention was in assembly and some members wanted to adjourn immediately, arm and march to the relief of The Alamo. But Sam Houston cautioned; the Convention must remain in session to form a government and he would find the troops and head off immediately.

Sam charged: "If mortal power would avail, I will avail the brave men in The Alamo."

For Sam Houston , the fall at The Alamo was an agonising nightmare and his instinctive reaction was to mount his battle horse and head straight for San Antonio.

With 783 auxiliary soldiers, hastily recruited, Sam Houston confronted Santa Anna and 1,800 Mexican troops at the Battle of San Jacinto on April 21, 1836. The odds were against them, but in only 20 minutes Houston's "Texians", charging to the cry "Remember The Alamo", were victorious. The Mexicans lost 630 soldiers killed and had 730 taken prisoner, among them the hated Santa Anna, who was first to humiliatingly concede independence for Texas in Houston's presence.

Santa Anna's life was preserved by Houston, the victor, and the Mexican leader was held as a hostage for peace.

The battle had been the great turning point for the Texans, who had just declared their independence and were certainly not in the mood for turning.

The militia men who fought under Sam Houston were of the type who fought the British to a standstill in the Revolutionary War two generations before.

They were settler farmers, unpaid and not professional soldiers, except for a few. They were raised by Houston only for the current emergency in the Texas lands that they had just recently moved to and, soon after routing the Mexicans, they began drifting gradually back to their farms. They had crops to get in, families to feed, chores of the utmost necessity to fulfil.

Santa Anna, after talks with his Texan captors, signed a treaty at Velasco in May 14, 1836, which pledged him personally never to take up arms against Texas.

It was also agreed that all hostilities between Mexico and Texas would cease immediately and the Mexican Army would withdraw below the Rio Grande River.

Santa Anna acceded for Mexico to achieve four things: diplomatic recognition of Texas; Texan independence; a treaty of commerce between the two nations, with the Rio Grande acknowledged as the Texan-Mexico boundary.

Sam Houston, injured in the right ankle at San Jacinto, headed to New Orleans for treatment, but by the autumn of that year he was back in Texas, by popular consent.

He became President of an independent Texas, taking the oath of office at Columbia on October 22, 1836, and serving two terms - 1836-38 and 1841-44, during which the economic prosperity of the fledgling republic made rapid progress.

Sam, celebrated by his men as "The Tallest Texan", was elected over Stephen Austin by an overwhelming majority of voters; Mirabeau Buonaparte Lamar was his Vice-President and the new Texas constitution was unanimously adopted.

In Washington, the Sam Houston-led triumph at San Jacinto was warmly welcomed by President Andrew Jackson, who had set his sights on United States expansion into Texas, beyond the Rio Grande. The defeat of Santa Anna and his Mexican army was celebrated ecstatically with parties by the Washington establishment.

Early in his Presidency, Houston managed to send the avowed enemy Santa Anna back safely to Mexico and a few months later he secured recognition of the new Texas Republic by the United States administration.

·᠗21᠘·

SAM HOUSTON'S
PRESIDENTIAL ASPIRATIONS

The 'Lone Star' Texas republic which Sam Houston presided over which largely a sprawling collection of frontier plantation settlements, consisting of about 40,000 subsistent farmers, most of whom had moved from Tennessee, Kentucky, the Carolinas and Virginia.

There were little or no economic structures in the region, no banks or organised schools. There was no industry. It was a raw frontier community in every sense, a throwback to the late 18th century when their forebears were settling the Appalachian region, with government authority very loosely organised.

In March 1846, Sam was elected as a United States Senator for Texas, which had been admitted to the Union four months earlier, and in this role he served 14 years.

In a speech on November 25, 1841, Sam Houston declared: "Texas has achieved her entire independence and has successfully asserted her right. How has this been accomplished? By the spirit and energy of her citizens - by the valour of her sons - by the inspired language breathed by her daughters."

During his United States Senatorship, Sam opposed the Southern state doctrine that Congress had no right to legislate on slavery in the territories. He also advocated California as a state of the Union and spearheaded the development of the Pacific railroad through Texas.

Towards the end his lengthy political career, Sam Houston became associated with the rapidly conservative Know-Nothing Party (electorally designated the American Party), which bitterly opposed foreign elements from a Roman Catholic background, particularly from Europe, who were increasingly gaining in influence and position in the Democratic Party, particularly in the northern east-coast states.

Sam left the Democratic Party and, for a time, he articulated these prejudices, an interesting phase in his political career considering that Sam had, for most of his life, been a very tolerant man, of all races and creeds.

The Know-Nothing Party phase for Sam lasted only a short period.

In 1854, he turned his sights towards an American Presidential nomination and for most of a year actively campaigned to achieve what his political mentor Andrew Jackson had achieved.

He delivered strong American nationalist speeches in cities and towns across the country; many rallied to his standard and, significantly, his tone was increasingly hostile to the Democratic Party.

A new Republican Party had just been formed and it threatened to become a serious challenger against the Democratic Party's hold on the Presidency.

When the American Party held its convention in February, 1856, however, Houston was surprisingly not considered as a serious Presidential candidate and the nomination fell to Milliard Filmore, a former President.

In the Presidential election which followed in November, Filmore was decisively defeated by James Buchanan, a Democrat from Lancaster County, Pennsylvania with very strong Scots-Irish family (Ulster) roots - his father had emigrated from Co. Tyrone.

In 1859, Sam, clearly disappointed at his failure in the Presidential bid, was still very much involved in politics but no longer in the national mainstream.

Sam was elected Governor of Texas as an Independent and he served until 1861, when on the enrolment of the state as a member of the Confederacy, he refused to take the necessary official oath and formally recognise the authority of the new Convention.

Passionately pro-Union, he resolutely refused to swear allegiance to the Confederacy and its cause. It was a momentous decision for him!

As a consequence, Sam Houston was unceremoniously forced out of office by the Confederate politicians, but he was now an old man, extremely war-weary and disillusioned and he did not resist the conservative political drift, apart from sending a message of protest at the illegality of his removal from office.

President Abraham Lincoln, a Republican, offered him the use of the United States Army to defend his position, but Sam wanted no more blood spilt among his own people - he favoured a peaceful solution.

He retired to his farm at Huntsville, Alabama and, after an illness lasting five weeks, died on July 26, 1863, aged 70, as the Civil War, he so greatly feared and detested, raged.

DECLARING FOR TEXAS

The unanimous Declaration of Independence made on behalf of the people of Texas in a general convention at the town of Washington on March 2, 1836 was signed by 58 delegates, including Sam Houston.

It declared: "The necessity of self-preservation now decrees our eternal political separation. We, therefore, the delegates with plenary powers of the people of Texas, in solemn convention assembled, appealing to a candid world for the necessities of our condition, do hereby resolve and declare, that our political connection with the Mexican nation has forever ended, and that the people of Texas do now constitute a free, Sovereign, and independent republic, and are fully invested with all the rights and attributes which properly belong to independent nations; and, conscious of the rectitude of our intentions, we fearlessly and confidently commit the issue to the decision of the Supreme arbiter of the destinies of nations."

SAM HOUSTON

DAGUERREOTYPE BY UNKNOWN PHOTOGRAPHER

·✧22✧·

SAM HOUSTON:

A SECOND MARRIAGE AND

THE FINAL YEARS

Sam Houston married a second time, in May 1840 to Margaret Lea, of Marion, Alabama, and they enjoyed a happy stable relationship, which produced eight children.

Margaret was the daughter of a Baptist pastor and it was her saintly influence which led to Sam's Christian "born again" conversion at Independence, Texas in 1854.

From being brought up in a solid Presbyterian/Calvinist family background, where some of his close relatives were devout Non-Conformist men of the cloth, Houston later experienced the heathen faiths of the Cherokees and, for a brief time in Mexico, the doctrines of Roman Catholicism, taking the baptismal name of "Paul". He was later highly critical of the arbitrary power of that church.

His strong addiction to drink, where at one stage in his early life he became known as "the Big Drunk", did not, however, endear him to committed church people during a considerable period of his career and, in the conservative establishment of early 19th century America, this may have halted his gradual progress in national politics to the lofty level of the Presidency.

After his conversion to the Baptist faith, Sam regularly corresponded with his wife when away from home, providing resumes of sermons he had heard preached. He joined the Sons of Temperance organisation, leaving far behind his excessive drinking habits from earlier years.

However, Sam spurned a request from a delegation of Texas church ministers, who asked him to use his influence in getting a Sunday alcohol prohibition law passed for the state.

After outlining his reasons, Sam added: "I am a sincere Christian. I believe in the precepts and examples as taught and practised by Christ and His Apostles to be the bedrock of democracy."

During the 1854 session of Congress, Sam made it known that he wanted to make a public confession of his religion, but decided that the best place to do this was in his home community in Texas, alongside his family and friends. In a revival mission at Independence, Texas, Sam was converted publicly and later baptised in Little Rocky Creek.

Sam often referred to his wife Margaret as "one of the best Christians on earth" and, significantly, his dying words - "Margaret, Margaret, Texas, Texas".

On the evening of his death on July 26, 1863 his beloved wife Margaret wrote in her family Bible her own personal tribute: "Died on the 26th of July, 1863, General Sam Houston, the beloved and affectionate husband, father, devoted patriot, the fearless soldier, the meek and lowly Christian".

Sam had been in failing health for a lengthy period. By the early part of 1863 his eyesight had nearly gone and he was being troubled by the wound he had sustained in military battles. He contracted pneumonia and becoming bedridden, he grew weaker and weaker in his last days.

A Texas newspaper report of Sam's death concluded: "To his numerous friends it will be doubtless a matter of great satisfaction to learn that in his last hours he was sustained by the Christian's hope and that he died the death of the righteous".

Sam made his will a few days before his death and in the fifth clause he said: "To my eldest son Sam Houston, I bequeath my sword, worn in the battle of San Jacinto, to be drawn only in defense of the constitution and laws, and liberties of his country. If any attempt be made to assail one of these, I wish it to be used in its vindication".

Houston, whatever his accomplishments as a politician, statesman and soldier, never acquired real wealth, to that attained by some of his contemporaries.

He was not good at finance management and economics and, although his estate at the time of his death listed 89,288 dollars in assets, very little of this was liquid cash and his widow Margaret experienced great difficulty in making ends meet after he died.

Indeed, it is recorded that Sam's funeral was unpretentious and sparsely attended, perhaps at his wife's wish. She had so little money that it was sometime before she could obtain a tombstone for the grave.

Sam Houston, for all of his remarkable achievements for nation and state, had quite a humble burial.

This fulsome tribute was paid to Sam Houston by 1960s United States President John F. Kennedy: "He was one of the most independent, unique, popular forceful and dramatic individuals ever to enter the Senate chamber. He was in turn magnanimous, vindictive, affectionate, yet cruel, eccentric yet self-conscious, faithful yet opportunistic.

"But Sam Houston's contradictions actually confirm his one basic consistent quality, indomitable individualism, sometimes spectacular, sometimes crude, sometimes mysterious, but always courageous".

His courage was undoubtedly fired and inspired by the unique Scots-Irish characteristic of his pioneering settler forebears from across the Atlantic who tamed the American frontier and created a civilisation.

Sam Houston was arguably one of the greatest Americans never to become the nation's President, but the Houston legend lives on, in the Tennessee and Texas territories which he helped make bastions for liberty, democracy and independence.

Houston was a man of many parts and American historian Ernest C. Shearer accurately described his moods: "He was as inconstant as a weather vane, solid as a rock, mercurial as a chameleon; intense as the heart of the sun, enthusiastic as a child, vain and proud as a peacock, humble as a servant, direct as an arrow, polished as a marquis, rough as a blizzard and gentle as a dove. In short, it was difficult to fit him to any set pattern".

William Johnson, in his book 'Sam Houston; Tallest Texan" (published in 1953), wrote that as far as the men who served under Sam Houston was concerned "there was no other general".

"His men regarded him as being as tall as a church steeple, but in reality he was only six and a half foot tall. More importantly, perhaps, Sam Houston had a way of thinking, talking and acting that made him seem a giant," William Johnson recorded.

The city of Houston in south-east Texas - named after Governor Sam Houston - was established in 1836, the year Texas Independence was declared. It was then a small community of ramshackle wooden buildings along perpetually muddy streets and it served briefly as the seat of government for the state.

In present-day Houston (population 2.2million), Sam Houston Park stands as a memorial and Sam's imposing statue is located at Hermann Park.

Of all the places Sam Houston lived in Texas, Huntsville was his favourite. This centre of education is home of the Sam Houston University. There is also a Sam Houston Memorial Museum in Huntsville.

At Independence, named in honour of the March 2, 1836 Declaration, the ruins of Baylor College, which Sam Houston helped to establish, still stands. Independence Baptist Church where Sam converted to the Baptist faith, is still in existence.

Washington-on-the-Brazos, where the Declaration of Independence was signed, has a re-creation of the orginal 1836 Independence Hall. Sam, a signer, was named Commander-in-Chief for the Republic after this signing.

Sam Houston Regional Library and Research Center is located at Liberty on land given by former Texas Governor Price Daniel and his wife Jean, a great-great grand-daughter of Sam Houston.

San Jacinto battleground State Historical Park at LaPorte is located 20 miles east of downtown Houston. This battle site marks the events of April 1836.

THE SAM HOUSTON LEGACY

1. In 1850, 18,000 native Tennesseans lived in Texas, the largest contribution to the region from any other state in the Union and, obviously, this was largely due to the patriotic influence of Sam Houston; legendary frontier associates David Crockett and Jim Bowie and other pioneering spirits who came South to seek land and opportunity in a state that was expanding as no other in the United States.

2. Sam Houston was a highly prolific letter writer and the manuscript materials of his life's work are abundant and widely scattered across the United States. The chief Houston collections are assembled in Austin, at the University of Texas.

3. Sam Houston, like his political mentor President Andrew Jackson, was a member of the Masonic Order and he helped organise Lodges in both Tennessee and Texas. Sam became a member of the Cumberland Masonic lodge No 8 in Nashville when he was 24. He affiliated with Holland Lodge No 1 in Houston, Texas in 1837 and, at that time, was a member of the Grand lodge of Texas.

4. Sam Houston was elected to the United States Congress from the state of Tennessee in 1823 and in a letter from Andrew Jackson to former President Thomas Jefferson the Houston credentials were confirmed.

The letter, written by Andrew Jackson from his Hermitage, Nashville home on October 4, 1823, read:

"This will be handed to you by General Samuel Houston, a representative to Congress from this state and a particular friend of mine to whom I beg leave to introduce you.

"I have known General Houston many years, and entertaining for him the highest feelings of regard and confidence, recommend him to you with great safety.

"He has attained his present standing without the intrinsic advantages of fortune and education and has sustained in his various promotions from the common soldier to Major General the character of the high-minded and honorable man as such as I present him to you, and shall regard the civilities which you may tender him as a great favor.

"With a sincere wish that good health and happy days are still yours, I remain your friend and very obliged servant."

The letter is evidence of the close bond which existed between Sam Houston and Andrew Jackson and the influence Jackson had with Thomas Jefferson, the third United States President.

The original letter is from the Sam Houston Hearne Collection, Sam Houston Regional Library and Research Center, PO Box 310, Liberty, Texas 77575. The letter is reproduced courtesy of Robert L. Schaadt, the Center Director.

5. Sam Houston, like Andrew Jackson, was a slave owner and in 1843 spoke in support of slavery. In 1852, while a United States Senator, he wrote: "I would not hesitate to veto any bill impairing the law for the protection of constitutional rights which guarantee to the people of the South the possession and enjoyment of their slave property."

However, in 1842, when he was President of the Republic of Texas, Sam proclaimed a treaty between Texas and Great Britain for the suppression of African slave trade.

At the outbreak of the Civil War in 1861, he was not prepared to accept the sessionist or slavery group in the Southern states.

The sword which Sam Houston left in his will to his son Sam Jnr. was bequeathed, as he said, "to be drawn only in defense of the Constitution, the laws and liberty of this country".

24

ELIZABETH PAXTON HOUSTON:
MOTHER OF AN AMERICAN LUMINARY

Elizabeth Paxton Houston, mother of Tennessee and Texas Governor Sam Houston, was made of a steely resolve required for the arduous frontier life in the Shenandoah Valley of Virginia and in East Tennessee during the late 18th century and early 19th century.

This mother of nine children - six sons and three daughters, Sam was the fifth child - was a member of a Scots-Irish family - the Paxtons, who, like the Houstons, moved from the north of Ireland to America during the mid-18th century.

Elizabeth was a very devout Presbyterian, who according to records of the time was "gifted with intellectual and moral qualities" above that of most women on the frontier. It was said her life was characterised by "purity and benevolence".

During the Revolutionary War, Sam Houston's father Sam had served as captain, paymaster and later major in Morgan's Rifle Brigade, a crack unit of the American patriot army and in 1783 he married Elizabeth Paxton, a daughter of one of the richest men in the Shenandoah Valley.

Sam Snr. inherited his father's farm at Timber Ridge outside Lexington and they worshipped at Timber Ridge Presbyterian Church along with other Scots-Irish settler families - the Paxtons, Davidsons, Stuarts, McCorkles, McCormicks, Lyles, McClungs and Montgomerys.

The Timber Ridge Church was built in 1746, several hundred yards from the Houston home, and a thriving congregation is still in existence today, carrying on the Calvinist faith and the cultural legacy that they had inherited from the first Scots-Irish settlers.

Sam Houston left a detailed description of life among the early immigrants in the Shenandoah Valley of Virginia.

He recalled: "Their cabins had but one door and no windows except holes between the logs and the light shone down from the top of the log chimney. Their bedsteads . . . mostly cross-sticks with thick clapboards on which were laid skins of bears and buffaloes.

"Their food consisted chiefly of venison, bear meat, buffalo, raccoon, turkey, pheasant, the river fish and eels, Irish potatoes, pumpkins, wild turnips and cabbages. Their bread was coarse Indian corn meal made in wooden morters by wooden pestles. Some had pewter basins, plates and tankards, but most persons, used trenchers and platters - made . . . out of tallow poplar wood".

Sam remembered with affection his father's "squared log house with its glass windows, which was the admiration and wonder of the neighbors".

The Houstons of the Shenandoah Valley did have a certain affluence, and influence on society there!

A grammar school was established at Timber Ridge in1749 by a Robert Alesxander, a leading member of the Presbyterian congregation, known as Liberty Hall, and later to become the Washington and Lee University, one of the foremost educational institutions in Virginia.

When her husband Sam, a major in the Virginia militia, died in 1807 on a tour of frontier army posts, Elizabeth Houston, then aged 52, moved with her family from the Shenandoah Valley in two covered Conestoga wagon train to Maryville, Blount County in the Great Smoky Mountains of East Tennessee.

There, they settled on land which Sam Snr. had purchased with the intention of moving closer to kinsfolk who had settled in East Tennessee.

They worshipped at Baker's Creek Presbyterian congregation and twice and often three times a week Elizabeth and the children walked in all weathers the four miles over the hills to services. They were also attached to New Providence Presbyterian Church in Maryville.

Sam and his brothers helped their mother erect the log cabin home on a 419-acre site at Maryville, at a point close to a river which divided the settlements of the white settlers from the lands of the Cherokee Indians.

The land was cleared, the house was built and the crops were planted, in typical late 18th and early 19th century frontier style and, with the children grouped all around her, Elizabeth proved a redoubtable industrious citizen of Maryville and its environs, even taking a keen interest in the business affairs of the town by opening a grocery and hardware store.

Elizabeth Houston had shown remarkable courage and determination in moving the large family household such a distance after the death of her husband. She was a woman of big build and forceful personality, qualities that stood her in good stead in the male-dominated world of the stark Virginia-Tennessee frontier.

Elizabeth Houston's sound Christian counseling was an obvious influence on young Sam and in his later life he admitted that the early impressions passed on by her far outlived all the wisdom of his adult life.

Sam adored his mother - she had nursed him from a serious injury he had received during a battle with the Indians - and on the little finger of his left hand he wore a ring which she had given as a young man. The ring had the word 'Honor' engraved on it.

Sam, in one of his nostalgic moments in 1859 four years before his death and long after his mother had passed on, said: "Sages may reason and philosophers may teach but the voice which we heard in infancy will ever come to our ears, bearing a mother's words and a mother's counsels".

The renowned early 19th century soldier, statesman and politician was a complex man who did not always live up to the fine Christian principles set by his mother, but he did, however, end his days as a Baptist convert, largely through the steadying influence of his second wife Margaret Lea.

In August 1831, Sam Houston was involved in important land treaty talks with the Indian tribes when he heard that his mother was very ill and dying. He rushed immediately to Maryville in East Tennessee to be with her and arrived just in time.

Elizabeth Paxton Houston was in her last hours and it was a defining moment in Sam's life as the woman who had most influenced him left the scene of time.

THE SELF-RELIANT SCOTS-IRISH

French historian Amuary De Riencourt, in a fascinating critique of the Scots-Irish, described them, thus: "They were strong, inhumanly self-reliant, endowed with an ecstatic dryness of temper which brushed aside the psychological complexities of mysticism, these puritans were geared for a life of action.

"They shunned objective contemplation and were determined to throw their fanatical energy into the struggle against nature.

"They fought their own selves with gloomy energy, repressing instincts and emotions disciplining their entire lives . . . Remorselessly brushing all men who stood in their path."

BENJAMIN FRANKLIN, speaking in 1784 on Scots-Irish control of the Pennsylvania government, said: "It is a fact that the Irish emigrants and their children are now in possession of the government of Pennsylvania, by their majority in the Assembly, as well as of the great part of the territory; and I remember well the first ship that brought any of them over."

"The Scots-Irish who came to America in the 18th century had a pride which was a source of irritation to their English neighbors. It was said of a Scots-Irishman that his looks spoke out that he would not fear the devil should he meet him face to face."

Sketches of some of the First Settlers of Upper Georgia by GEORGE R. GILMER.

A 19th century American historian provided a vivid description of the Scots-Irish frontier settlers with the following passage:

"Thus the backwoodsmen lived on the clearings they had hewed out of the everlasting forest; a grim, stern people, strong and simple, powerful for good and evil, swayed by gusts of stormy passion, the love of freedom rooted in their hearts' core.

"Their lives were harsh and narrow; they gained their bread by their blood and sweat, in the unending struggle with the wild ruggedness of nature. They suffered terrible injuries at the hand of the red man and on their foes they waged a terrible warfare in return.

"They were relentless, revengeful, suspicious, knowing neither ruth nor pity; they were also upright, resolute and fearless, loyal to their friends and devoted to their country.

"In spite of their many failings, they were of all men the best fitted to conquer the wilderness and hold it against all corners."

·2·5·

CROCKETT CHRONOLOGY:

TIME LINE

1600s: largest concentration of Crocketts around Coupar (Cupar) Angus, East Central Scotland.

1600s: the Plantation of Ulster - migration to Co. Tyrone and Co. Donegal.

1688-89: Crocketts defend Londonderry for the Protestant cause in the Siege of the city.

1708: Crocketts (Joseph Louis and his wife Sarah Stewart) settle in Pennsylvania, probably around Chester County.

1716: Joseph Louis Crockett takes his family to Virginia.

1748: Crockett family reside in Frederick County near Winchester, Virginia.

1768: Crocketts move to Lincoln County, North Carolina.

1771: Names of Dacid Crockett (David's grandfather) and two of his sons are written in the records of Lincolnton Court House, North Carolina.

1776: Crocketts leave Lincoln County for Hawkins County, North Carolina (now North East Tennessee).

1777: November - David Crockett's grandparents massacred by Cherokee Indians near their cabin at Rogersville, Tennessee. David's father John was not at home when the attack took place. His uncle Joseph was wounded; his uncle James was captured and was held captive for 20 years.

1780: October 7 - John Crockett marries Rebecca Hawkins and later that year he fought at the Battle of Kings Mountain, South Carolina.

1786: August 17 - David Crockett born in Greene County on the Nolichucky River at Big Limestone Creek, Tennessee territory.

1792: Family takes up residence five miles north-west near the home of Rebeckah Hawkins Crockett's brother Joseph Hawkins. The farm was 10 miles north-east of Greeneville, between Walkertown and Rheatown, Tennessee.

1794: Crocketts move to the mouth of Cove Creek near the Dulaney community mill disaster. John Crockett's mill at Cove Creek was washed away in a flood.

1795: Crockett family move to the rented tavern at Morristown, Tennessee.

1799: David, aged 13, starts and is punished by his father for playing truant, and he runs away.

1800-1802: David Crockett lives and works in Virginia, and for a period he worked in Baltimore.

1802: David Crockett goes to work at Panther Springs between Jefferson City and Morristown, Tennessee.

1806: August 12 - Marries Polly Finlay (Finley) and moves to Finley's Gap/ Bays Mountain, eight miles east of Dandridge, Tennessee.

1811: Lived on Mulberry Creek, a tributary of the Elk River, Middle Tennessee.

1812: moves to the area around Winchester in Middle Tennessee.

1813: David moves his family to Bean's Creek, Franklin County, Tennessee.

1812-14: David Crockett fought under Andrew Jackson in the Creek War.

1815: Polly Finlay Crockett dies and is buried at Bean's Creek, Franklin County, Tennessee, beside where they lived.

1816: David Crockett marries Elizabeth Patton.

1817: David Crockett lives at Shoal Creek, Lawrenceburg, Middle Tennessee.

1817: Became justice of the peace and lieutenant colonel of the local militia.

1818: David is elected colonel of the 57th Regiment of Militia in Lawrence County.

1821: David is elected to the Tennessee State Legislature for Lawrence and Hickman Counties.

1823: David is re-elected to the Tennessee State Legislature.

1827: David elected to the United States Congress (House of Representatives) for West Tennessee.

1830: David parts company with President Andrew Jackson over land and river issues. He also speaks out strongly in Congress against the Indian Removal Bill.

1831: David is defeated in his bid for re-election to Congress.

1833: David runs again for Congress and is re-elected.

1834: with the help of Thomas Chilton David writes and publishes his biography - 'A Narrative of the Life of David Crockett of the State of Tennessee'. David heads on a speaking tour of the eastern coastal states and New England.

1835: David is defeated again in a final bid to get re-elected to Congress. November 1 - David heads to Texas from his West Tennessee home.

1836: January 13 - David moves from San Augustine, Texas and reports for duty at Bexar, Texas under Colonel William Travis. January 15 - Last letter home to his daughter Mary (Polly). February 23, 1836 - moves to The Alamo and siege begins. March 5 - David Crockett's last reported memorandum from The Alamo. Sunday March 6 - David Crockett dies gallantly at The Alamo in Texas. March 23 - A report in the Telegraph and Texas register in Austin, Texas reports death of David Crockett and 188 others at The Alamo. April 21 - General Sam Houston's army routs General Santa Anna's Mexican forces at Battle of San Jacinto with the defiant battle cry "Remember The Alamo".

Early in the summer of that year, writer Richard Penn Smith compiles "Colonel Crockett's Exploits and Adventures in Texas".

1837: Over the year, a total of 45 Crockett almanacs are published in major cities in the United States by various publishers.

1845: December 29 - Texas becomes a state of the Union (the 28th).

Data part compiled by historian Joseph Swann, the Mayor of Maryville, Tennessee, and chronicleer on the early life of David Crockett and now the proud owner of David's treasured gun 'Old Betsy.'

DAVID CROCKETT'S BIRTHPLACE AT LIMESTONE, TN

26

DAVID CROCKETT:

THE EARLY YEARS

Gallant American frontiersman David Crockett died at The Alamo in Texas five months before his 50th birthday, but in his 49 years this rugged and independent-minded Tennessean lived life to the full and created a lasting legend and myth that lies right at the heart of folklore in the United States.

This highly colourful and courageous character, as he personally related in his autobiography, was born in a humble log cabin in a valley alongside the Big Limestone River and the Nolichucky River in Greene County, North Carolina (a region that was part of the lost state of Franklin and later to become part of the state of Tennessee) on August 17, 1786.

No records of his birth exist, but forget the Hollywood movie story that David was born on a mountain top in Tennessee - he was born in a holler, on low ground, beside a fast flowing tributary river that linked up with the Holston and Tennessee waterways.

Today, a marble slab marks the David's birthplace on the north bank of the Big Limestone River. There is also a replica of the family's wooden cabin and a visitors' centre, preserved and administered by the David Crockett Birthplace Association.

His parents were humble people of very little education, barely able to read and write, but they were typical frontier folk of the period, using their wits and commonsense to forge a living.

David himself progressed in his knowledge through the education of life in the wooden, mountain region of his beloved Tennessee. In his autobiography, he said of his parents - "They were poor and I hope honest".

He also wrote: "My father's name was John Crockett and he was of Irish descent. He was either born in Ireland or on a journey from that country to America cross the Atlantic.

"He was by profession a farmer and spent the early part of his life in the state of Pennsylvania. My mother was Rebecca Hawkins. She was an American woman, born in the state of Maryland, between Baltimore and New York."

Davy, who preferred to be called David, may have been a rural backwoodsman, but he had enough intelligence, commonsense and cunning to survive and outwit even his most devious adversaries and highly educated political opponents.

He was in every respect a man of the people - humble, straight-talking and honest, even quick-tempered - the fifth child of a close-knit family of nine (six sons and three daughters) born to John and Rebecca (Rebeckah) Crockett. His brothers were John, William, Thomas, James and Joseph and sisters Betsy, Jane and Sally.

David's father was a member of the Lincoln County militia in North Carolina and had fought in the Revolutionary War, at the Battle of Kings Mountain on October 7, 1780 with his brother Robert and six other kinsmen.

David was a romantic adventurer, explorer and hunter who left an indelible mark on the rugged landscape of his frontier homeland and the stories of his exploits and achievements will always be at the cornerstone of American life.

Crockett was also a soldier and politician of standing, as well as being a celebrated storyteller, folklorist and wit. He was a man with the common touch, someone who was fully aware of precisely where he had come from and where he was going (or where he wanted to go).

He was quick-tempered and assertive and these mannerisms invariably brought him into conflict with both adversaries and contemporaries.

A man, six feet in height and weighing 200 lbs, David Crockett was of great physical stature and bearing.

James Wakefield Burke, in his book David Crockett - The Man Behind the Myth, said David possessed the essential attributes for that abounding country.

"He was an adventurer, with a talent for falling in with strangers, a memory for names and faces, a gift of storytelling, inexhaustible ability for sharp-shooting, that freedom from conscience that springs from a contempt for pettiness and bureaucracy. He was a free soul and he sought only the company of those of like temperament.

"There seems to have been graven into this liberated man from the dirt farms of Tennessee a reluctance to be tied down, to be obligated for long to any engagement, to own anything save his Long Rifle. In whatever group he appeared he brought the glamour of the frontier," wrote Burke.

Before spending the last few months of his life in Texas, where he stood at The Alamo in March 1836 stoutly defending liberty and democracy for his country, David lived in at least seven different locations in Tennessee. He spent the first twenty five years in East Tennessee; the next ten in Middle Tennessee around Nashville and the last fourteen in the wild and sparsely-inhabited West Tennessee towards Memphis.

There is no evidence that David Crockett had a formal church connection in Tennessee, but his family were of Ulster Presbyterian stock when they left the north of Ireland for the 'New World' in the mid-18th century.

The Crocketts had arrived in America from the north of Ireland in the early 18th century, having lived in the Tyrone-Donegal counties in the province of Ulster after moving there from lowland Scotland during the 17th century Plantation.

The family may originally have been French Huguenots, a Protestant community who were driven out of France in the 17th century by the Roman Catholic administration there.

David Crockett is the great, grandson of William Crockett, a brother of Joseph Louis Crockett and his grandfather David passed through the Shenandoah Valley, verified by the fact that his son Robert was born at Barryville in the region in 1755.

By 1771, the Crocketts were in North Carolina with deed records of Tyron County confirming David Snr. had bought a 250-acre farm on the south side of the Catawbe River close to Charlotte in North Carolina. They also lived at Lincolnton in Western North Carolina.

Within a few years, the family had moved to the Holston River valley in the Tennessee lands, and formed a settlement in Carter's Valley where the town of Rogersville now stands. This became known as Crockett's Creek

In November 1777, David Crockett's grandparents were massacred in a Cherokee Indian attack on their homestead at Carter's Creek as the Crocketts were putting in crops on their land space.

There, within a radius of three miles David Crockett Snr. and three of his sons John, William and Joseph lived on separate farmlands. David's father John was away at the time of the killings, but his uncle Joseph, who was reportedly deaf and mute, was taken captive and did not return home for 17 years.

The massacre, marked on a gravestone in a old cemetery in the centre of Rogersville, a town founded by Cookstown, Co. Tyrone man Joseph Rogers, left the small clutch of Scots-Irish families in the region fearful and very vulnerable.

It was a chilling, frightening experience, but the Crocketts and their Scots-Irish settler neighbours re-grouped to form a cohesive defensive strategy to combat the threat posed by frequent Indian attack.

The Rogersville cemetery inscription on the decaying Crockett headstone reads: "Here lies the bodies of David Crockett and his wife, grandparents of Davy Crockett, who were massacred within their cabin near this spot in 1777."

David Crockett, in his autobiography of 1834, wrote: "By the creeks, my grandfather and grandmother were both murdered; in their homes and at the very spot of ground where Rogersville, in Hawkins County, now stands."

Despite his limited education, John Crockett had been a magistrate, land speculator and one-time tavern owner. His wife Rebecca Hawkins, who was born in Maryland, also reached North Carolina via the Shenandoah Valley with her Scots-Irish family and she and John eventually settled at Limestone Creek in Greene County.

In his 1836 autobiography (A Narrative of the Life of David Crockett of the State of Tennessee), David said of his parents: "They were poor, and I hope honest".

27

DAVID CROCKETT:

ON THE MOVE IN TENNESSEE

David Crockett spent the first five years of his life at Limestone Creek. The family moved to Cove Creek where his father had a partnership in a mill, but it was a short stay as, disastrously, the mill and the Crockett home were destroyed in a flood.

The next stop was Morristown in Jefferson County, Tennessee, where John Crockett opened a tavern on the main road from Abingdon in Virginia to Knoxville. It was effectively a wagon station where settlers and drivers stopped overnight, resting themselves and their stock.

The family later had a tavern at Morristown in East Tennessee, another typical frontier town of the late 18th century inhabited by a significant number of Scots-Irish settlers.

When he was twelve, David was hired out as a cattle hand to a Dutch settler Jacob Silver in Rockville, Virginia. He found the work rewarding, but was homesick and trekked the 400 miles home, only to be sent back to school by his father.

But the classes only lasted four days and, fearing punishment at home for his truancy, he finally decided to make his way in the wider world.

David tried a succession of jobs over a three-year period, and after passing through Virginia, worked for a time at Baltimore docks. He was employed for six months by a Quaker John Kennedy, who allowed him to attend educational classes. But Davy preferred the freedom to roam the forests and mountains of his rugged and wild Tennessee homeland, as a fearless hunter living and working off the land.

David's first love was a young Scots-Irish lass from the region called Margaret Elder and, while the pair went as far as to take out a marriage licence in 1805, they eventually went their separate ways.

On August 12, 1806, however, David, then aged 19, married pretty 17-year-old Polly Finley (Finlay), who was also Scots-Irish on her father's side, and, while Polly's mother was looking for better for her daughter than the intrepid, restless Crockett, the marriage blended with three children to their name - sons John Wesley and William and daughter Margaret Polly.

The couple lived for a few years on a rented farm near the home of Polly's father in Jefferson County, but the going was hard and they moved west into Middle Tennessee, beyond the Cumberland Mountains.

By 1811, they had settled at Mulberry Creek, on the Duck and Elk Rivers in what is now Moore County. The surrounding forests were rich in deer and smaller game, the ideal spot for a man of David Crockett's tastes and adventurous spirit.

Within two years, Davy moved the family to Bean Creek in Franklin County, to a home called 'Kentuck' and stayed there until after his involvement in Andrew Jackson's war with the Creek Indians in 1812-14, when he saw action in Alabama and Florida.

Crockett originally volunteered for 90-day service in the Second Regiment of Volunteer Mounted Riflemen, but the military duties were extended and he was selected as a scout to spy on the Indian territories, along with a close friend George Russell. It was during this expedition that David gained the reputation of being a bear hunter, with his trusty Kentucky Long Rifle.

David joined the regular army and fought the Indians at Fort Strother and Fort Taladega and encountered British forces in Andrew Jackson's Florida campaign.

He was a third sergeant in Captain John Cowen's company in the War of 1812. Later, he served as lieutenant in the 32nd Militia Regiment (Franklin County) and as colonel of the Lawrence County Militia Regiment. It was in this latter service upon which Crockett's title of colonel was based.

Around this time, Polly Crockett took ill at her Mulberry Creek home and David had speedily to return home to take care of her and the young children.

Polly had always been a delicately frail person and the many moves and natural hardship she faced on the frontier wilderness sapped her energy and strength.

She died in the summer of 1815 leaving a distraught and highly confused David to look after the three young children and for a time a younger brother and his wife helped out.

David loved Polly greatly, but within a year, he married again, to a widow Elizabeth Patton, the mother of two children whose husband had been killed in the Creek War.

Elizabeth was also of Scots-Irish origin, of a good family background from North Carolina, and her sizeable farm helped David to increase his social status. Widowed twice, Elizabeth came to Texas in 1854 and died there in 1860, aged 72.

David, despite having taken on another wife and two more children, continued to hunt and explore and with neighbouring settlers he looked over the Alabama territory, which had just been acquired from the Creek Indians. On that mission, he contacted malaria and was fortunate to get home alive.

David later took advantage of the Treaty of 1816 with the Chickasaw Indians and found another settlement at Shoal Creek near Lawrenceburg in Middle Tennessee.

Within two months, he was a justice of the peace and town commissioner and he later became lieutenant colonel of the local militia. His new found civic duties, on his own admission, were seriously taxing his educational abilities, but he claimed that he got by on his "natural born sense", rather than any knowledge of the law and government procedures.

DAVID CROCKETT

COURTESY OF THE TENNESSEE STATE LIBRARY
AND ARCHIVES, NASHVILLE

28

DAVID CROCKETT:
PUBLIC REPRESENTATIVE IN
TENNESSEE AND AT WASHINGTON

David was elevated to colonel in the militia and in 1821 was elected to the Tennessee state legislature for Lawrence and Hickman counties. While electioneering, he admitted he had never read a newspaper and knew nothing about government, but he had talents as a soap box orator and a humour which endeared him to ordinary grassroots voters.

Crockett was also a gifted storyteller, but for all his natural instincts and talents, he was looked down on by representatives of the moneyed classes and slightingly referred to as "the gentleman from the cane". But David knew his constituency and the poor backwoods families rallied to his cause.

While attending the Tennessee legislature at Murfreesboro, David's large grist powder mill and distillery on Shoal Creek were swept away in a flood - a repeat of the misfortune which struck his father at Cove Creek - and he was forced to move the family to Rutherford Fork, 150 miles distance.

He was re-elected to the legislature in 1823, defeating Dr William E. Butler, a nephew of Rachel, the wife of Andrew Jackson and one of the region's most wealthy men.

Butler had education, money and influence, but Crockett had the uncanny knack of persuading voters over on to his side.

In his accounts, David tells of a special hunting short which he wore when campaigning. It was of buckskin, outsize and had two pockets. In one pocket, he carried whiskey and in the other tobacco.

David reckoned that when he met a prospective voter he would treat him first with whiskey and before leaving him he would hand him a twist of tobacco to replace the "chaw" he had disposed off when he took the drink.

The reason was that if a man was in good humour, in as good a shape as when he found him, the vote was secure on polling day. Butler was routed at the polls and Crockett returned to represent five Tennessee counties.

The David Crockett life motto was "going ahead" and in the early years of his bid to gain political recognition this appeared to become a reality.

David Crockett was, in many respects, a socialist, although he espoused the capitalist free market ideals of the American dream. The major issue for the 1823 legislature was the disposition of lands belonging to the state and the mopping up of the territory formerly under the control of North Carolina in the late 18th century.

Crockett, who was joined in the debate by President-to-be James Knox Polk (another of Scots-Irish family roots), deeply mistrusted the federal government over its legislation on the territorial state remits of Tennessee and North Carolina.

David, who had two terms as a Tennessee state legislator, also opposed legislative handling of divorce cases and he had numerous run-ins in debates with Andrew Jackson, shortly to become President. Perhaps, their confrontational Scots-Irish characteristics and natural sense of destiny were so similar that conflict was inevitable!

Later as a Congress man, Crockett irked the Washington establishment when he put forward a resolution to abolish the nation's celebrated military academy at West Point.

His main argument was that only the sons of the rich and influential could get into West Point and that the bounty of the Government should go to the poor rather than to the rich. He contended that the War of 1812 had shown that a man could fight the battles of his country and lead his country's armies, without being educated at West Point; as shown by the success of Andrew Jackson. who had since progressed to the highest office in the land.

In 1827, David (after an unsuccessful bid in 1825 when he lost by only two votes) was elected to the United States Congress for West Tennessee, defeating General William Arnold and Colonel Adam Alexander, who both dismissed the Crockett bandwagon convinced it was a straight fight between them. David won by 2,748 votes and he held the seat at the next election.

However, Crockett's opposition to Andrew Jackson's Indian Bill prevented him getting another term. His attitude was: "I am at liberty to vote as my conscience and judgment dictate to be right, without the yoke of any party on me, or the driver at my heels, with the whip in his hands, commanding me 'gee-whoa-haw' just at his pleasure".

David was very much his own man, even in the presence of more powerful company, and once when after an usher at President Jackson's home at the Hermitage in Nashville one evening announced: "Make way for Colonel Crockett", there came the reply: "Colonel Crockett makes room for himself" - unceremoniously and unpretentiously entering into the presence of the President.

Although he fought alongside Andrew Jackson in various battles, David parted company with the President over land and river issues that greatly affected the livelihoods of his people in the backcountry.

Crockett said in March, 1830: "To General Jackson, I am a firm and undeviating friend. I have fought under his command . . . I have loved him . . . and still love him; but to be compelled to love everyone who . . . for self-aggrandizement pretend to rally around the 'Jackson Standard' is what I can never submit to. The people . . . ought to look for breakers! The fox is about; let the roost be guarded".

David and other Tennessean representatives were disappointed at President Andrew Jackson's stand against financial aid for the improvement in the transportation facilities of the state.

David strongly believed in human rights, including those of the native American people, and he led opposition to Andrew Jackson's Indian policy of forcing the Indian tribes living east of the Mississippi River to move to the western part of the Louisiana territory, and indeed later to Oklahoma.

When the bill approving the measure at a cost of 500,000 dollars was put before Congress in 1830, David was the only Tennessean to vote against it. His main objective was that he did not want to see the poor remnants of "a once powerful people" forced to move "against their will".

David represented four counties in West Tennessee on the border of the Chickasaw Indian country and he was appalled at the decision, with the consent of the President, to drive these native tribes west of the Mississippi to lands in Oklahoma.

He also knew that many the now-peaceful Cherokees would prefer "death in their homes" to moving away from their ancient and natural environment in Tennessee.

During his last term in Congress, David toured major eastern cities and New England states and, wherever he went, he was met by huge crowds and great ovations.

The man from the Tennessee cane was in big demand as a speaker at banquets and dinner parties and when he visited Philadelphia he was presented with his famous rifle 'Betsy'. This bore the gold and silver inscription: "To the honorable Davy Crockett of Tennessee by the young men of Philadelphia".

At this stage in his political career, David Crockett was even being considered as a serious contender by the Whig element in Washington to oppose the Presidency of Martin Van Buren, the hand-picked candidate of Andrew Jackson in 1836.

But this prospect disappeared when, largely due to the influence of Andrew Jackson and Tennessee Governor William Carroll, David lost his Congress seat to Adam Huntsman, a lawyer with a wooden leg.

Crockett became totally disillusioned with politics and caustically he remarked: "Since you have chosen to elect a man with a timber toe to succeed me, you can all go to hell and I will go to Texas."

His last surviving letters spoke of his confidence that Texas would allow him to rejuvenate his political career and finally make his fortune. David planned to become a land agent in Texas and he saw his future in an independent territory that was compatible with his own ambitions.

The gun 'Betsy' was to accompany David on his last fateful journey to Texas for the battles with the Mexicans - and, nostalgically, the trusted weapon was recovered by his family after the fall at The Alamo.

29

DAVID CROCKETT:

THE TRAIL TO TEXAS, AND THE ALAMO

David Crockett left his West Tennessee home for Texas on November 1, 1835, three months after his election defeat for Congress. His political career was over and the tremendous urge to explore new territory had again seized him.

His aim was to improve his economic well-being on the Texas frontier. He told contemporaries: "You can go to hell, I'm going to Texas".

The straight-talking David moved to Texas via Memphis down the Mississippi River through Arkansas and into the Red River Valley. This verged on Comanche Indian country where the tribes were on the warpath, as menacing to the American settlers as the Mexicans under their President, General Antonio Lopez de Santa Anna.

Soon after his arrival in Nacogdoches, David took the oath of allegiance to the provisional government of the independent Republic of Texas, which was being led by his old associate and contemporary from the early Tennessee years - Sam Houston.

Tensions, however, existed between David Crockett and Sam Houston, largely because of the political fall-out David had with President Andrew Jackson in Congress.

After David's death, however, Sam Houston in a tribute described his fellow Tennessean as "a brave, honest and gallant spirit".

On the momentous trek to Texas, Crockett was joined by his nephew William Patton, who had accompanied him to Texas in an initial 17-strong party which was to be become known as the Tennessee Mounted Volunteers.

Texas was in revolt against the ruling junta in Mexico and the stakes were high as both sides prepared for a fight to the death. Crockett and his men reported for duty at Bexar on January 13, 1836 and they were warmly welcomed by Colonel William Travis, who, because David also bore the title of Colonel, offered him command of the fort. Crockett refused, stating he had come to defend Texas as a private.

When word came through on February 11 that Santa Anna and a large Mexican army had crossed the Rio Grande into Texas, it was decided that all the men of the Texas garrison should go as soon as possible into the enclosure of The Alamo, an old walled Franciscan mission station in what today is the centre of the city of San Antonio.

The movement into The Alamo was not completed until February 23 and it was there over the next few weeks that 189 men, together with some women, children and black servants, were to take refuge from the advancing 5,000-strong Mexican army led by Santa Anna.

Most of the volunteers including Crockett, were Tennesseans - David brought an entourage of 12 rifles; the rest were Kentuckians and Virginians. They were all enthusiastic volunteers and none were to receive pay for their service.

Among them was a Tennessean of Scottish roots, Colonel Jim Bowie, the man credited with inventing the Bowie knife, although he fully realised it was going to take much more than the several hundred men recruited to defend the garrison. He believed they needed 1, 000 men to make it secure from the impending Mexican attack

Illness from tuberculosis prevented Jim Bowie from taking an active role in the battle. Colonel William Travis, aged only 25, was in command and he kept repeating even at the height of battle: "Victory or death! I shall never surrender or retreat!"

Sam Houston, like Crockett of Ulster-Scots extraction, was major-general of the regular army in the new independent republic of Texas, but it was an army which had still to be recruited. The siege lasted 13 days and, while guns were fired daily at sunrise to alert army reinforcements, it was to no avail.

The siege began on February 21, 1836 and Crockett's pledge to Colonel Travis was "Colonel, here I am. Assign us a position and I with my Tennessee boys will try to defend it".

The "boys" were the twelve Tennesseans and they were assigned to the most vulnerable point at the station. Crockett, always a man with a destiny, considered the calling at The Alamo an honour and he set about making the most of what was to turn out to be a totally hopeless situation.

In a memorandum dated February 23, Crockett wrote: "Early this morning the enemy came in sight, marching in regular order. They'll find that they have to do with men who will never lay down their arms as long as they can stand on their legs".

Ominously, in another recorded message on March 3, David Crockett declared: "We have given over all hope of receiving assistance from Goliad or Refugio".

Eighteen cannon were mounted as the siege began and Colonel Travis in his report said: "The Hon. David Crockett was seen at all points animating the men to do their duty".

The accurate rifle fire of the Tennesseans kept the Mexicans at bay, but time and supplies were running out. And there was no sign of the army reinforcements that had been promised by Sam Houston and others in military forts in other parts of Texas.

A detachment of 32 men arrived on March 1, but two days later there came the news from a courier that 400 men had turned back because of difficulties on the way and, because the officers felt another Texas station was more in need of defending than The Alamo.

Santa Anna decided the fort should be taken by assault and the first two charges were beaten back with huge losses on the part of the Mexicans. In a third assault, concentrating on the north wall of the fort, the Mexicans managed to breach the defences and gain access to the plaza of the mission.

The Texans were outnumbered and had to retreat to the buildings around the plaza and the mission church. Their cannons were seized and used to batter down the doors. The defenders took their last stand in hand-to-hand combat and many died at the receiving end of a Mexican bayonet.

An estimated 189 Texans were killed, with their bodies placed on a funeral pyre and burned. The only survivors were non-combatants, mostly Mexican women and children, several black slaves of Colonel Bowie and Colonel Travis, and a Mrs Dickinson, wife of an officer at the garrison.

Various accounts of how David Crockett died at The Alamo have been rendered. It is claimed he was one of six survivors who surrendered to Santa Anna and was shot dead on the Mexican leader's orders. But it is generally accepted that he fell behind the south wall, which he and the Tennesseans were charged to defend. Mrs Dickinson, who was led from the church, said in her testimony: "As we passed through the enclosed ground in front of the church I saw heaps of dead and dying. I recognised Colonel Crockett lying dead and mutilated between the church and the barrack building and even remember seeing his peculiar cap lying by his side".

Two slave witnesses, Santa Anna's cook Ben and Colonel Travis's servant Joe, claimed Crockett's body was surrounded by Mexican corpses. Ben reported seeing David's knife buried "up the hilt in the bosom of a Mexican found lying across his body".

It was said that Crockett fought to the end, killing many Mexicans. His last act of helpfulness was loading Jim Bowie's rifle and pistol. Reportedly, his last words were "Boys, aim well!"

General Sam Houston found the fall of The Alamo an agonising nightmare. Ironically, Sam was presiding at a convention at Washington in Texas dealing with the independence of Texas and, when word reached him of the last message ever dispatched by Colonel Travis, he walked out, mounted his battle horse and, with three companions, headed for The Alamo.

The party rode hard all day, only stopping when their wearied horses could go no further. He knew that the signal gun would be fired as long as The Alamo held out. The last one was fired on the day that he had read Travis's message (Sunday March 6) - the day the Mexicans butchered most of the 189 men.

Sam Houston was too late to render assistance at The Alamo, but through his leadership, and, against all the odds, he managed to retrieve the position for the Texan cause in the days that followed.

The Alamo, by restricting Santa Anna's army for two weeks, had allowed the Texan army to get organised. The battle cry had now become "Remember the Alamo" and, under Sam Houston, the Texans, heavily outnumbered but determined to "save Texas", won a famous victory at the Battle of San Jacinto.

It was 700 brave, but largely untrained Texas against 1,800 Mexicans, and, buoyed by the frenzied cries of "The Alamo", Houston's men won the day in 20 minutes.

The Mexicans had 630 killed and 730 prisoners were taken, including their commander Santa Anna. The Texan losses were eight killed and 23 injured.

Houston, who suffered an ankle injury, secured from Santa Anna a treaty recognising Texas independence and, by September of that year, he was

President of the new republic. Texas later became a state of the Union - the 28th - on December 29, 1845.

The Telegraph and Texas Register in Austin reported in its issue of March 24, 1836: "The end of Davy Crockett of Tennessee, the great hunter of the west, was as glorious as his career through life had been useful. He and his companions were found surrounded by piles of assailants, whom they immolated on the altar of Texas liberties.

"The countenance of Crockett was unchanged: he had in death that freshness of hue, which his exercise of pursuing the beasts of the forest and the prairie had imparted to him. Texas places him, exultingly, amongst the martyrs of her cause".

John Wesley Crockett, David's son, who later represented his father's old constituency of West Tennessee in the American Congress and was re-elected twice, wrote to his uncle George Patton, of North Carolina: "You have doubtless seen the account of my father's fall at The Alamo in Texas. He is gone from us and is no more to be seen in the walks of men, but in his death like Sampson (Samson) he slew more of his enemies than in all of his life.

"Even his most bitter enemies here, I believe, have buried all animosity and joined the great lamentation over his untimely death".

As a politician, John Wesley Crockett succeeded where his father had failed in Congress by obtaining a land bill upholding the interests of settlers in the backcountry.

Like his father, John Wesley Crockett died a young man; he was just 45 when he suddenly passed away in Memphis in 1852, having lived most of his life in West Tennessee.

In addition to his political role in Washington, he was a lawyer and also a highly reputed journalist and edited various publications in New Orleans. His wife Martha was the daughter of Judge John C. Hamilton.

David Crockett's last reported memorandum, written on March 5, 1836 carried the words: "Go ahead, liberty and independence forever!"

Military strategists may look back on The Alamo as a disaster - that a significant body of soldiers were allowed to be surrounded by a force vastly superior in numbers, but it is widely accepted that the supreme sacrifice made by David Crockett and the others in the little mission station largely contributed to securing independence for Texas.

Shortly after The Alamo, John Wesley Crockett went to Texas to retrieve his father's rifle 'Betsy' and, with other personal belongings, the weapon became a treasured possession in the family, being handed down from generation to generation.

David Crockett once wrote: "I'll leave the truth for others when I'm dead. First be sure you are right and go ahead".

Obviously this was a man in the highest traditions of his Scots-Irish family heritage. The legend and myth of David Crockett was indeed for real.

* There are 17 historical markers relating to David Crockett across the state of Tennessee. A county in Texas is named Crockett County, in honour of the redoubtable frontiersman.

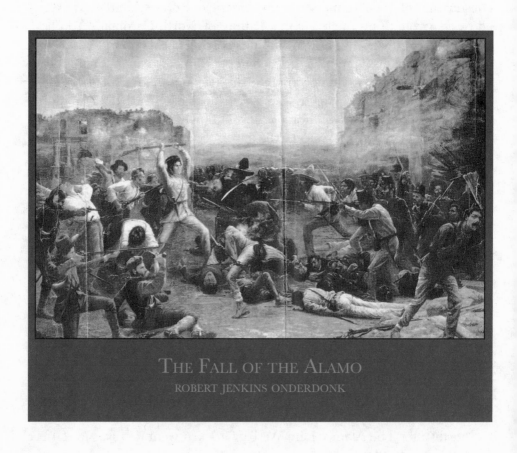

THE FALL OF THE ALAMO
ROBERT JENKINS ONDERDONK

30

DAVID CROCKETT:
HIS LAST LETTER HOME

Seven weeks before David Crockett's death at The Alamo he wrote his last letter. The letter, written from Saint Augusteen in Nacogdoches, Texas on January 9, 1836, was to his daughter Mary (Polly or Margaret) and her husband Wiley Flowers at Gibson County, Tennessee.

The letter makes very interesting reading and is a last personal testimony before David, aged only 49, met his terrible fate with 188 others at the hands of a ruthless Mexican army under General Santa Anna in the little Alamo mission station at San Antonio in the days leading up to and on March 6, 1836.

"My dear sons and daughter. This is the first time I have had the opportunity to write you with convenience. I am now blessed with excellent health and am in high spirits.

"I have got through safe and have been received by everybody with the open ceremony of friendship. I am hailed with a hearty welcome to this country. A dinner and party of ladies have honored me with an invitation at Naching Docher (Nacogdoches).

"The cannon was fired here on my arrival and I must say as to what I have seen of Texas it is the garden spot of the world, the best land

and the best prospects for good health I ever saw and I do believe it is a fortune to any man to come here.

"It's not required here to pay down for your league of land. Every man is entitled to his head right of 400-420 acres.

"They may make the money to pay for it on the land. I expect in all probability to settle on the border of the Red River, that I have no doubt is the richest country in the world.

"There is a world of country here to settle, the richest country in the world. Good land, plenty of timber and the best springs and good mill streams, good range of clear water . . . game aplenty.

"It is the path where the buffalo passes from north to south and back twice a year, and bees and honey plenty. I have a great hope of getting the agency to settle that country and I would be glad to see every friend that I have settled there.

"I have taken the oath of government and have enrolled my name as a volunteer for six months and will set out for the Rio Grande in a few days with the volunteers from the United States.

"But all volunteers is entitled to a vote for a member of the convention or to be voted for, and I have but little doubt of being elected a member to form a constitution for this province

"I am rejoiced at my fate. I had rather be in my present situation than to be elected to a seat in Congress for life.

"I am in hopes of making a fortune yet for myself and family, bad as my prospect has been. I hope you will all do the best you can and I will do the same. Do not be uneasy about me. I am among my friends.

"I will close with great respects."

Your affectionate father, Farewell, David Crockett.

31

A Daughter's Recollections
of a Father

David Crockett had three children - Robert, Rebecca E. and Matilda - by his second marriage, to Elizabeth Patton, whose first husband had been killed by Indians at the battle of Horseshoe Bend during the Creek War.

A newspaper interview, given by Matilda Fields (David's daughter) about 1882, provide some explanation as to why Crockett went to Texas as he did in 1835.

"I was born in Lawrence County, Tennessee August 2, 1821. Father was twice married. His first wife was Miss Mary Finley, by whom he had three children - John Wesley, William and Margaret.

"I remember distinctly the morning he started out on his journey to Texas. He was dressed in his hunting suit, wearing a coonskin hat cap, and carried a fine rifle presented to him by friends in Philadelphia.

"He was a large fine portly looking man, and loved to hunt and shoot at matches. A few days before he started in his fatal trip he gave a big barbecue and barn dance, and everybody far and near were invited.

"A great many people were there. They had a glorious time. The young men danced all day and night and everybody enjoyed themselves.

"People used to come from a distance and stay several days with father hunting and sporting. I remember the day father came home after his last race. He came in and said to mother: 'I am beat, I am off to Texas.'

"I don't think father cared much for his defeat; he wanted to go to Texas anyhow.

"He wanted to move right away, but mother persuaded him to go first and look at the country and then if we liked it we would all go.

"He seemed very confident the morning he want away that he would soon have us all to join him in Texas. We did not know that he was going into the Texas war when he went off. We did not know that he intended to go into the army until he wrote mother a letter after he got to Texas.

"We were all greatly distressed when we heard that he had been killed; we could hardly believe it".

Matilda (Crockett) Field, in the interview, said that when her brother moved to Texas her mother went with him and settled on land given to her by the state of Texas. She only lived about six years afterwards.

"Father spent much of his time hunting, electioneering or at Washington city, that it seems now like I was never with him much," she said.

This transcript, from a West Tennessee newspaper, was found in a box of possessions belonging to Dollie M. Crockett, daughter of Robert Patton Crockett, who was the only son and oldest child of David Crockett's marriage to Elizabeth Patton. The article subsequently was in the possession of Carol J. Campbell, the great-great-great grand-daughter of David Crockett. John Wesley Crockett, David's son, was a journalist for a period during the later part of the 19th century with a newspaper in Dover, Tennessee.

Permission to use the information in this book was given by Joy N. Bland, of Paris, Tennessee, the historian of the direct descendants of David Crockett and kin.

"No man can make his name known to the forty millions of this great and busy republic who has not something very remarkable in his character or in his career. But there is probably not an adult American, in all these widespread States, who has not heard of David Crockett. His life is a veritable romance, with the additional charm of unquestionable truth. As such, his wild and wondrous life is worthy of the study of every patriot."

John C. Abbott 1874

·32·

DAVID CROCKETT:
THE ABSORBING STORYTELLER,
RACONTEUR AND MUSICIAN

For essentially a self-educated man with very little formal schooling, David Crockett was remarkably a prolific writer who for most of his adult life penned letters to friends and associates and, a short time before he died, he even wrote his own biography.

The autobiography, titled 'A Narrative of the Life of David Crockett in the State of Tennessee', was published in 1834 with the help of an aide Thomas Chilton. This became a best-seller.

The authentic book countered many of the earlier outlandish tales which featured in Sketches and eccentricities of Colonel David Crockett, of West Tennessee, although these stories were provided by David himself, with some embroidering and tongue in cheek observation.

Crockett was a romantic who liked to listen to and to tell tall tales around the camp fires or holed up in his long cabin, or in the company of politicians of like mind in more auspicious surroundings in Washington.

These stories became legend across America and beyond, and they have been perpetuated long after his untimely death at The Alamo in March 1836.

The Crockett jovial and genial personality centred mostly around story-telling, but he also liked to sing and dance and it was said his fiddle playing provided an entertaining musical interlude for folks in the bleakness of early 19th century American frontier life.

Crockett's own journals tell of his last fateful days at The Alamo in Texas in February and March 1836:

February 23 - "Early this morning the enemy came in sight, marching in regular order. They will find they will have to do with men who will never lay down their arms as long as they can stand on their legs."

March 3 - "We have given over all hope of recovering assistance from Goliad or Refugio (Texas garrisons)."

March 5 - "Pop, Pop, Pop! Boom, Boom, Boom! Throughout the day. No time for memorandums now. Go ahead! Liberty and independence forever."

In a chapter titled 'Last Days at The Alamo' (from the book 'David Crockett's Own Story'), David cited prose which summed up their gallant quest for freedom and independence by Americans, like himself:

"Up with your banner Freedom,
The champions cling to thee;
They follow where'er you lead them,
To death or victory;
Up with your banner, Freedom.

"Tyrants and slaves are rushing,
To tread thee in the dust;
Their blood will soon be gushing,
And stain our knives with rust,
But not thy banner freedom.

While stars and stripes are flying,
Our blood we'll freely shed;
No groan will 'scape the dying,
Seeing thee o'er his head;
Up with your banner, Freedom".

David Crockett, in another poignant lament penned in 1835 just after finishing his final term as a Congressman in Washington and before he moved to Texas and The Alamo, wrote:

"Farewell to the Mountains whose mazes to me
Were more beautiful far than Eden could be;
No fruit was forbidden, but Nature had spread
Her bountiful board, and her children were fed,
The hills were all garners, - our herds wildly grew,
And nature was shepherd and husbandman too.
I felt like a monarch, ye thought like a man,
As I thanked the Great Giver and worshipped His plan.

"The home I forsake where my offspring arose;
The graves I foresake where my children repose.
The home I redeemed from the savage and wild:
The home I have loved as a father his child.
The corn that I planted, the fields that I cleared,
The flocks that I raised, and the cabin I reared;
The wife of my bosom - Farewell to ye all!
In the land of the stranger I rise and or I fall.

"Farewell to my country! I fought for thee well,
When the savage rushed forth like the demons from hell.
In peace or in war I have stood by thy side,
My country for thee I have lived, would have died!
But I cast off - my career now is run,
And I wonder abroad the prodigal son
Where the wild savages rove, and the broad prairies spread,
The fallen - despised - will again go ahead!"

David's literary expertise was exceptional for someone from such a humble background at that time, with a very limited education, and living and hunting most of the time, as he did, in the wilds of the desolate Tennessee frontier lands during the early 19th century.

He personally described himself as "a plain, honest, homespun writer" and his distinctive style endeared itself to legions of fellow Americans

Scores of books and almanacs were compiled in the years immediately after David Crockett's death and more than 20 actors have played the part of Crockett in films, the earliest being Charles K. French in 1909.

Two classic Hollywood movies 'Davy Crockett: King of the Wild Frontier'(1954) starring Fess Parker as the hero.

'The Alamo' (1960), with John Wayne also in the role of David and Richard Widmark as Jim Bowie, perpetuated in true American style the memory of the celebrated Tennessee frontiersman and his sturdy compatriots.

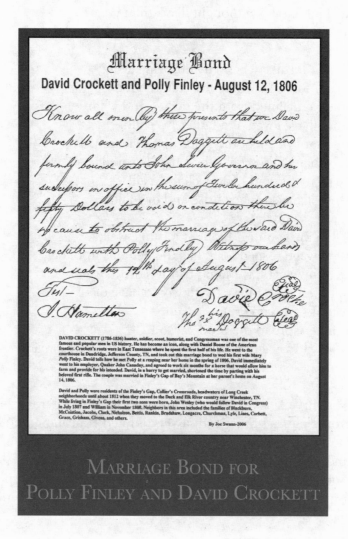

MARRIAGE BOND FOR
POLLY FINLEY AND DAVID CROCKETT

33

MARY POLLY FINLAY (FINLEY), WIFE TO DAVID CROCKETT

The mother of pretty Mary Polly Finlay (Finley), a Scots-Irish lass from East Tennessee, had ambitions that her daughter would marry a husband more settled and of greater substance than the intrepid David (Davy) Crockett, who was keeping her company.

Polly's love, however, for this highly colourful and courageous frontiersman overcame her mother's doubts and, in a short but reasonably happy marriage which lasted almost ten years (1806-15), the couple flitted from various homes, through East and into Middle and West Tennessee.

Polly's parents were both of Scots-Irish immigrant families and her father William had been on expeditions with Daniel Boone in the Carolinas and Kentucky.

From first sight, David, who had earlier courted another young Scots-Irish woman Margaret Elder, was in love with Polly and he admitted that he was "plaguy well pleased with her from the word go".

David was just a week short of 20 and Polly a few years younger when they married on a licence issued in Dandridge Courthouse in East Tennessee on August 12, 1806 and the marriage was solemnised a few days later by a preacher after a few traditional frontier customs were observed.

David's brothers and a few friends approached the Finlay home on his behalf with an empty jug. If Polly's father filled it up, this was the sign that he approved of the marriage and to Davy's delight the match was made when his friends came back with a pitcher overflowing. A wedding gift was two cows with calves!

The Crockett marriage produced three children, sons John Wesley and William and daughter Margaret Polly, but life was exceedingly difficult in the wooded wilderness of the Tennessee frontier for delicate and frail Polly.

Davy was for ever roaming the Tennessee forests and the mountains, leaving Polly alone for long periods with the children. It was a lonely, at times bleak existence in the inaccessible rural hills of Tennessee in the early 19th century.

For the first few years of the marriage, they lived on a small rented farm at Bay's Mountain in Jefferson County, East Tennessee near Polly's father's Finlay's Spring Creek settlement, but they struggled to make end's meet and Davy was convinced their best hope was to move west to more fertile land.

Polly, it was said, kept a comfortable home within the meagre means and David could at least feed her and the children from his hunting in the forests and rivers, but there was little or no money to pay the rent, much less for the bare necessities of a home.

In 1811, they made the long 150-mile trek over the Cumberland Mountain plateau and took up residence at an attractive spot near the headquarters of Mulberry Creek, a branch of the Elk River at Maury County in Middle Tennessee.

David and Polly then moved to territory straddling Franklin County and Lincoln Tennessee, near the Alabama state line, to eventually set up a home at Bean's Creek, near the present-day town of Winchester, which they called "Kentuck".

There, on the Mulberry fork of the Elk River tributary of the mighty Tennessee River, Davy marked his initials on a beach tree and laid out a five-acre claim on state land, and built a cabin home. This was great hunting country and David was able to indulge his passion as never before.

Unfortunately, the many home moves in Tennessee and the natural hardship Polly faced during cold and wet winters on the frontier sapped her energy and strength and, several months after giving birth to daughter Margaret, she died a very young woman in her late twenties, leaving David to care for three very small children.

Before Polly's death, David had been soldiering as a "mounted gunman" in the American Army, battling with the Creek Indians at Fort Strother and Fort Taladega and encountering British troops in the Florida campaign, and, it was on leave for the birth of the third child that he found her in sickly condition.

No definite cause of death was established and historians say it may have been either typhoid or cholera. The illness, in the summer of 1815, lasted several weeks and when she died, a distraught David buried her on a hill near the cabin at Bean's Creek in Franklin County, Tennessee.

The gravestone, erected by the Tennessee Historical Commission, remembers Polly thus: "Polly Finlay Crockett. Born 1788 in Hamblen County. Married to David Crockett August 12, 1806. Mother of John Wesley Crockett - 1807. William Crockett - 1809. Margaret Finlay Crockett - 1812. Died 1815."

Polly Finlay was very close to David Crockett's heart and it was said by associates that he "ever after" held the memory of his "tender and loving wife".

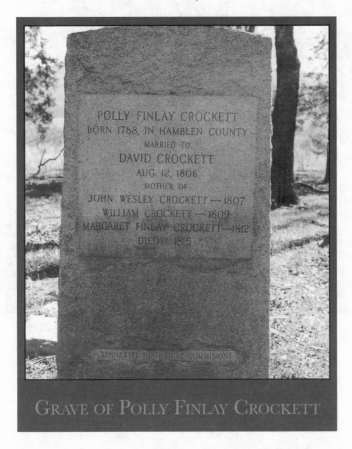

GRAVE OF POLLY FINLAY CROCKETT

141

CROSSROADS TO DESTINY
BY DAVID WRIGHT

RIGHT TO LEFT, ANDREW JACKSON, SAM HOUSTON
AND DAVID CROCKETT

34

THE LEGACY OF DAVID CROCKETT

1. Davy Crockett is remembered at his Limestone cabin birthplace at Greene County in East Tennessee alongside the Big Limestone and Nolichuckey Rivers thus: "Pioneer, Patriot, Soldier, Explorer, State Legislator, Congressman. Martyred at The Alamo. 1786-1836".

2. 'Old Betsy', David Crockett's favourite gun, is now the property of Joseph A Swann, Mayor of Maryville, Tennessee, and is located at the McClung Museum, Knoxville, under the trusteeship of the East Tennessee Historical Society.

A TRIBUTE TO DAVID CROCKETT:

"Too much has been made over the details of how DAVID CROCKETT died at The Alamo. Such details are not important. What is important is that he died as he had lived. His life was one of indomitable bravery; his death was a death of intrepid courage.

"His life was one of whole-hearted dedication to the concepts of liberty. He died staking his life against what he regarded as intolerable tyranny.

"A poor man who had long known the devastating consequences of poverty and who all his life had fought a dedicated fight for the right of the dispossessed to a new opportunity; he died defending a poor and insecure people and proclaiming their right to participation in the arts of self-government.

"This is the true significance of the birth and re-birth of DAVID CROCKETT."

From David Crockett: the Man and the Legend by James Shackford. Published 1956. Pages 238-239.

"I never had six months education in my life. I was raised in obscurity without either wealth or education. I have made myself to every station in life that I ever filled through my own exertions"
— David Crockett August 18, 1831.

"The adventures of David Crockett are commemorated at forty-nine sites in ten States throughout the United States. Crockett, as a frontiersman, huntsman, soldier and politician, was a restless, adventurous soul who kept on the move, starting his life in East Tennessee, and ending it in tragedy at The Alamo."

The David Crockett Birthplace State Park is situated near Limestone and the Greene County/Washington County line in East Tennesseee, about 11 miles from the town of Greeneville (the former home of President Andrew Johnson) and 12 miles from Jonesborough, the oldest town in Tennessee.
A furnished replica cabin and an engarved steeping stone from the originaol cabin can be seen at the park.
Limestone Creek and the Nolichuckey River flows adjacent to the park, which is a very popular site for holiday-makers and campers.
A walking trail leads to a waterfall and a small museum at the visitors' center includes displays about David Crockett's life on the Western American frontier and the early period that he lived through.

35

THE ROLL OF HONOUR
AT THE ALAMO

A total of 189 men, mostly frontier pioneering Americans, died at The Alamo in March 1836 fighting for the freedom and liberty of Texas.

David Crockett and Jim Bowie were the most high profile individuals who perished in what was a virtual impossible situation; many others were guys who had followed Crockett to Texas from Tennessee, Virginia, Kentucky and the Carolinas in the pursuit of the ideals of freedom and independence through the staking out of new homelands.

Nine of those killed were Irish born, mostly in Ulster, with a significant number first, second and third generation away from Scots-Irish pioneering forebears who crossed the Atlantic on emigrant ships through the 18th century.

The siege from Mexican forces started on February 23, 1836 when 5,000 troops led by General Antonio Lopez de Santa Anna surrounded the little mission station in the centre of San Antonio, which was bravely manned by the defenders under the command of Colonel William Travis.

The defenders saw The Alamo as the key to the defence of Texas and their independence and they were ready top give their lives rather than surrender to Santa Anna. The odds were stacked against them, but they considered it their duty to stand and fight.

The 13-day siege ended at sunrise on March 6 when the Mexicans mounted the walls of the fortress in waves of desperate hand-to-hand fighting and, after overwhelming the Texas by sheer numbers, they rushed the compound and seized control of the station.

The 189 Alamo heroes, officially listed by the Daughters of the Republic of Texas in San Antonio as gallantly laying down their lives on the Texas side, were:

A - Juan Abamillo (born San Antonio, Texas), Robert Allen (unknown) Miles DeForest Andross (unknown), Micajah Autry, (born North Carolina).

B - Juan A. Badillo (born San Antonio, Texas), Peter James Bailey (born Kentucky), Isaac G. Baker (born Arkansas), William Charles M. Baker (born Kentucky), John J. Ballentine (unknown), Richard W. Ballentine (born Scotland), John J. Baugh (born Virginia), Joseph Bayliss (born Tennessee), John Blair (born Tennessee), Samuel B. Blair (born Tennessee), William Blazeby (born England), James Butler Bonham (born South Carolina), David Bourne (born England), James Bowie (born Tennessee), Jesse B. Bowman (unknown), George Brown (born England), James Brown (Pennsylvania), Robert Brown (unknown), James Buchanan (born Alabama), Samuel E. Burns (born Ireland), George D. Butler (born Missouri).

C - Robert Campbell (born Tennessee), John Cain (born Pennsylvania), William R. Carey (born Maryland), Charles Henry Clark (born Missouri), M. B. Clark (unknown), Daniel William Cloud (born Kentucky), Robert E. Cochran (born New Jersey), George Washington Cottle (born Tennessee), Henry Courtman (born Germany), Lemuel Crawford (born South Carolina), David Crockett (born Tennessee), Robert Crossman (born Massachusetts), David P. Cummings (born Pennsylvania), Robert Cunningham (born New York).

D - Jacob C. Darst (born Kentucky), John Davis (born Kentucky), Freeman H. K. Day (unknown), Jerry C. Day (born Missouri), Squire Daymon (born Tennessee), William Dearduff (born Tennessee), Stephen Dennison (born England), Charles Despallier (born Louisiana), Almaron Dickinson (born Tennessee), John H. Dillard (born Tennessee),

James R. Dimpkins (born Tennessee), Lewis Dewall (born New York), Andrew Duvalt (born Ireland).

E - Carlos Espalier (born San Antonio, Texas), Gregorio Esparza (born San Antonio, Texas), Robert Evans (born Ireland), Samuel B. Evans (born Kentucky), James I Ewing (born Tennessee).

F - William Fishbaugh (born Alabama), John Flanders (born Massachusetts), Dolphin Ward Floyd (born North Carolina), John Hubbard Forsythe (born New York), Antonio Fuentes (born San Antonio, Texas), Galba Fugua (born Gonzales, Texas), William K. Furtleroy (Kentucky)

G - William Garnett (born Tennessee), James W. Garrand (born Louisiana), James Girard Garrett (born Tennessee), John E. Garvin (unknown), John E. Gaston (Kentucky), James George (unknown), John Calvin Goodrich (born Tennessee), Albert Calvin Grimes (born Georgia), Jose Maria Guerrero (born Laredo, Texas), James G. Gwynne (born England).

H - James Hannum (unknown), John Harris (born Kentucky), Andrew Jackson Harrison (unknown), William B. Harrison (born Ohio), Charles M. Heiskall (born Tennessee), Joseph B. Hawkins (born Ireland), John M. Hays (born Tennessee), Patrick Henry Herndon (born Virginia), William Daniel Hersee (England), Tapley Holland (unknown), Samuel Holloway (born Pennsylvania), William D. Howell (born Massachusetts).

J - William Daniel Jackson (born Ireland), Thomas Jackson (born Kentucky), Green V. Jameson (born Kentucky), Gordon C. Jennings (born Connecticut), Jimenes Ximenes (born Texas), Lewis Johnson (born Wales), William Johnson (born Pennsylvania), John Jones (born New York).

K - Johnnie Kellogg (unknown), James Kenney (born Virginia), Andrew Kent (born Kentucky), Joseph Kerr (born Louisiana), George C. Kimbell (born New York), Willam P. King (born Texas).

L - William Irvine Lewis (born Virginia), William J. Lightfoot (born Virginia), Jonathan J. Lindsay (born Illinois), William Linn (born Massachusetts), Toribio D. Losoya (born San Antonio, Texas).

McC - Edward McCafferty (unknown), Jesse McCoy (Tennessee), William McDowell (Pennsylvania), James McGee (born Ireland), Robert McGregor (born Scotland), Robert McKinney (born Tennessee).

M - George Washington Main (unknown), William T. Malone (born Georgia), William R. Marshall (born Tennessee), Albert Martin (born Tennessee), Eliel Melton (born Georgia), Thomas R. Millar (born Virginia), William Mills (born Tennessee), Isaac Millsaps (born Mississippi), Edward F. Mitchusson (born Virginia), Napoleon B. Mitchell (unknown), Edwin T. Mitchell (unknown), Robert B. Moore (born Virginia), Willis Moore (born Mississippi), Robert Musselman (born Ohio).

N - Andres Nava (born San Antonio, Texas), George Neggan (born South Carolina), Andrew W. Nelson (born Tennessee), Edward Nelson (South Carolina), James Northcross (born Virginia), James Nowlan (born England).

P - George Pagan (born Mississippi), Christopher Parker (born Mississippi), William Parks (born North Carolina), Richardson Perry (born Texas), Amos Pollard (born Massachusetts).

R - John Purdy Reynolds (born Pennsylvania), Thomas H. Roberts (unknown), Isaac Robinson (born Scotland), James Robertson (born Tennessee), James M. Rose (born Virginia), Jackson Rusk (born Ireland), Joseph Rutherford (born Kentucky), Isaac Ryan (born Louisiana).

S - Mial Scurlock (born North Carolina), Marcus J. Sewell (born England), Manson Shied (born Georgia), Cleveland Kinlock Simmons (born South Carolina), Andrew H. Smith (born Tennessee), Charles S. Smith (born Maryland), Joshua G. Smith (born North Carolina), William H. Smith (unknown), Richard Starr (born England), James E. Stewart (born England), Richard L. Stockton (born Virginia), A. Spain Summerlin (born Tennessee), William E. Summers (born Tennessee), William D. Sutherland (born Alabama).

T - Edward Taylor (unknown), George Taylor (unknown), James Taylor (unknown), William Taylor (born Tennessee), B. Archer M. Thomas (born

Kentucky), Henry Thomas (born Germany), Jesse G. Thompson (born Arkansas, John W. Thompson (born North Carolina), John M. Truston (born Pennsylvania), Burke Trammel (born Ireland), William Barrett Travis (born South Carolina), George W. Tomlinson (born Missouri), James Tylee (born New York), John (negro - unknown)

W - Asa Walker (unknown), Jacob Walker (unknown), William B. Ward (born Ireland), Henry Warnell (born Arkansas), Joseph G. Washington (born Tennessee), Thomas Waters (born England), William Wells (born Georgia), Isaac White (born Kentucky), Robert White (unknown), Hiram J. Williamson (born Pennsylvania), William Wills (unknown), David J. Wilson (born Scotland), John Wilson (born Pennsylvania), Anthony White (born England), Anthony Wolfe (born England), Claiborne Wright (born North Carolina).

Z - Charles Zanco (born Denmark).

Ten days (February 24, 1836) before the final surrender of The Alamo, Colonel William Barrett Travis, the commander at the besieged fort, sent this message:

"To the people of Texas and all Americans in the world; fellow Citizens and Compatriots. I am besieged by a thousand and more of the Mexicans under Santa Anna.

"I have sustained a continual bombardment and cannonade for 24 hours and have not lost a man. The enemy has demanded our surrender at discretion, otherwise the garrison are put to the sword if the fort is taken.

"I have answered the demand with a cannon-shot and our flag still waves proudly from the walls.

"I shall never surrender or retreat. Then I call upon you the name of Liberty, of Patriotism, and everything dear to the American character, to come to our aid with all dispatch.

"The enemy is receiving reinforcements daily and will no doubt increase to three or four thousand in four or five days.

"If this call is neglected and I am determined to maintain myself as long as possible and die like a soldier who never forgets what is due to his own honor and that of his country.

Victor or Death!"
— William Barrett Travis.

Daniel William Cloud, a Kentuckian compatriot of David Crockett and one of the fallen heroes at The Alamo, proclaimed on December 25, 1835, on route to Texas: "If we succeed, the country is ours. It is immense in extent and fertile in its soil and will amply reward all our toil. If we fail, death in the cause of liberty and humanity is not cause for shuddering. Our rifles are by our side, and choice guns they are; we know what awaits us and are prepared to meet it."
How prophetic his words were!

THE ALAMO
SAN ANTONIO, TEXAS

·~36~·

'BIG FOOT' WALLACE
AND HIS TEXAS CONQUESTS

Another gallant Scots-Irishman who fought with distinction against the Mexican and Indians in the San Antonio region of Texas in the 1830s and 1840s was William Alexander Anderson Wallace, from the Shenandoah Valley of Virginia.

Wallace, known as "Big Foot", was a Texas Ranger, hunter and adventurer, the great grandson of an Ulster Presbyterian couple Peter and Elizabeth Woods Wallace and his memory is perpetuated on a bronze statue in the centre of Lexington, Virginia.

The statue bears the inscription: "Big Foot Wallace 1817-1899. William Alexander Wallace was born one mile south of the corner marker of a brick house still standing which was near the dwelling of his grandfather Samuel Wallace, where the first Rockbridge Court was held in 1778.

"At the age of 23 he want to Texas in 1837 to avenge the death of his brother, who was massacred by the Mexicans at Goliad. A cousin also died at Goliad.

"Wallace served his adopted state as an Indian fighter, Ranger, Civil War soldier and post carrier, enduring great hardship and ordeals recorded in history. His remains are interred in San Antonio and the state of Texas has signally honored his memory. Wallace motto - Sperandum. Erected by his Virginia and Texas admirers. 1935."

"Big Foot" was a trouble shooter, operating from a San Antonio base. He would gather up small parties of men to cover a radius of 40 miles from San Antonio wherever hostile Indians were reported and his function was to meet danger head on. He had many violent run-ins with the Indian tribes and fought the Mexicans at the battle of Meir.

More than 600 Mexicans were killed at Meir, but with rations running out the Texans surrendered and Santa Anna ordered every man to be shot.

His governor Francisco Mexia, however, disobeyed and ordered every tenth man to be shot. A jar was filled with white beans and 17 black beans. The seventeen prisoners who drew a black bean were executed on March 25, 1843.

While many of the remaining prisoners died in captivity, Wallace was one of the few to escape and he lived to fight in the Mexican-American war and later joined the Texas Rangers.

When peace was declared, Wallace, also known as "Cap", acted a a guard or escort to the postal stage line carrying the mail between San Antonio and along the Rio Grande through old Fort Franklin, now El Paso city and Albuquerque, New Mexico.

The guards of the stage rode on horseback alongside the stage through very dangerous territory inhabited by Indian and Mexican bandits.

Wallace's great, grandmother Elizabeth Woods Wallace emigrated from the north of Ireland with her six children, five sons and one daughter, and four brothers and their families after her husband Peter died in 1724.

They settled at Lancaster County Pennsylvania and moved to Rockbridge County in the Shenandoah Valley of Virgina in 1739.

The Wallace family spread out from Virginia to Kentucky and Indiana and relatives of "Big Foot" were David Wallace, a Governor of Washington territory, and General Lew Wallace, Governor of New Mexico and a leading American author.

General Wallace fought in in the Civil War and he served on the court martial for Abraham Lincoln's assassin John Wilkes Booth.

37

THE ORIGINS OF THE SCOTS-IRISH

Scottish lowlanders who left Scotland for Ulster between 1610 and 1690 were biologically compounded of many ancestral strains. While the Gaelic Highlanders of that period were (as they still are) overwhelmingly Celtic in ancestry, this was not the case with the Lowland inhabitants.

The Lowlander had long since become a biological mix, in which nine strains had met and mingled in different proportions. Three of the nine were present in Scotland in pre-Roman days: the Stone Age aborigines; the Gaels, a Celtic people who overran the western part of the British Isles, and the Britons, another Celtic folk whose arrival pushed the Gaels north into Scotland and west to Wales.

Roman, Teutonic, Scots, Norse, Norman and Flemish influences were also brought to bear over a period of 1,000 years on the biological mix of a people that were to become known as the Scots-Irish.

Dourness was the most obvious characteristic of the lowland Scots. The word derives from the Latin "durus" and the French "dur", which literally means hardness and durability, having the qualities of iron. Men and women who survive centuries of living in a harsh environment, both physical and social, learn how to endure the worst that live can inflict on them. Such were the lowland Scots.

The Scots knew famine, and plague, thin soil, insecurity of life and poverty, raids and aggression. They learned to fight back, to give blow for blow, and, when they had done their best, to endure.

From the beginning of man, the Scots had a reputation of not being prepared to submit to any authority except their own. And this was shown in the Scottish homeland, in Ulster and on the American frontier lands.

Lowland Scots lived for their freedom, the freedom to live life as traditional Scots, with no man saying nay to their familiar rights. They did not tolerate subservience, there was nothing automatic about the loyalty a Scot showed to his chief although pragmatism and canniness were the attributes of both. The Scottish Lowlander has long been regarded as notoriously argumentative.

This trait developed after the Protestant Reformation as theological points were debated over for hours in the Presbyterian Kirk. The educational system which the Presbyterian Kirk introduced became the cornerstone of life in Scotland and the twin pillars of church and school were to lay the foundations of society for the Scots-Irish when they moved to Ulster and thence to America.

The Presbyterian tradition of church and school dates back to the teachings of Scottish reformer John Knox, who in his first Book of Discipline in 1560, instructed that "everie severall churche have a school maister", and that each father (minister or elder) in a congregation be compelled no matter what his "estair or condition", to bring up his children in "learnying and virtue".

Renowned Anglican bishop the Rev Gilbert Burnet, while on a tour of Scotland in the late 17th century, was much impressed by the Presbyterian regard for education. He was surprised to find even "a poor communality" able to dispute fine points of secular and sacred government and was even more surprised to find knowledge "among the lowest of them, their cottagers and servants".

So it was in Scotland, in Ulster and in America where the Presbyterians settled. Economic deprivation, caused by tighter landlord control on the leases of their tenant farmers, forced many Scottish Lowlanders to participate in the Plantation of Ulster from 1610.

This came about against a background of poverty, lawlessness and insecurity in Scotland and, after the first 30 years of the Plantation, an estimated 40,000 lowland Scots were located in the various counties of Ulster, with the figure multiplying in the years that followed.

Religious upheaval continued in Scotland for 100 years after the Reformation, and tensions increased when the Scottish Stuart kings moved to Westminster to also embrace the English throne.

James V1 of Scotland, the son of Mary Queen of Scots and later to be known as James 1, was not enamored by the Presbyterian form of worship. He believed the teachings of the Kirk, by its authority and freedom of speech, was a menace to the monarchical principle. England, he felt, had ordered its Protestant Reformation better by retaining bishops and a church hierarchy.

Throughout his reign, James 1 tried to impose Anglican guidelines on Presbyterians, without success. He undertook even to "correct" John Knox's hallowed Book of Common Prayer, so that it might be brought nearer the English Book of Common Prayer.

His son Charles 1, who ruled from 1625-49, shared his father's ideas about imposing English form of worship on the Scots, but he was just as frustrated in his attempts. And on Charles's execution in 1649, Oliver Cromwell tried to impose his Commonwealth form of government on the Scots, but they remained opposed and some paid for it with their lives when the Cromwellian forces headed north.

Charles 11 was an even more ruthless monarch as far as the Scots were concerned. He was determined to bring the Presbyterian Scots to heel and, within two years of ascending the throne, he had begun a campaign to drive from their pulpits those ministers who would not conform to the ways of the episcopacy.

There followed in Scotland what was known as "the Killing Times" when the resolute and fierce Covenanters of the western lowlands fought guerrilla warfare against Charles's men.

Refusing to accept episcopacy and, determined to worship God after their own accord, they left the towns to hold their meetings on hillsides and in secluded valleys.

They carried arms to defend themselves against the soldiers sent to hunt them down. Many were killed on the moors, hundreds were cast into prison, others tortured and some were hanged. But nothing could tame their spirit, their Reformed dissenting beliefs remained.

Events like the Battle of Bothwell Bridge in 1679, where the Covenanters were beaten, but not totally vanquished, stirred the nation and the Covenanters found an honoured place in Scottish history.

Many Covenanters fled to America, settling in South and North Carolina, while others joined their fellow countrymen in Ulster with their numbers greatly strengthening the Presbyterian elements in the Province. Presbyterians about the middle of the 17th century became dominant in five Ulster counties

- Antrim, Down, Londonderry Tyrone and Donegal - and they far outnumbered the English Anglican settlers there.

Population movements in both directions between Scotland and Northern Ireland have gone on for most of 2,000 years.

The sea journey between Ulster and western parts of Scotland is at its shortest 15 miles and longest 50 miles, and at most the peoples of the two countries are never more than a few hours sailing time, less than an hour in flying time.

38

THE RAW COURAGE OF
A PROUD PEOPLE

Scots-Irish immigrants from Ulster who settled in their thousands on the American frontier over the 18th century showed exceptional heroism in their quest for a new life and homeland

The courage and the raw courage shown by this dogged, determined people in very difficult circumstances helped shape the fabric and character of the United States as an embryonic nation and, ultimately, as the world power it is today.

Forging a civilisation out of a wilderness was a real challenge for those who landed on American shores in different waves 200-250 years ago, and they succeeded in moulding a decent, law-abiding society, from the eastern New England seaboard states, into the Appalachian region, south to Texas and Mississippi and west towards California on the Pacific coastline.

The Scots-Irish heroes, and the heroines - the sturdy womenfolk who made the family, the home and Christianity the cornerstone of frontier life - are enshrined in American history, not just United States Presidents, statesmen, soldiers and churchmen, but the many plain ordinary citizens whose quiet, unselfish deeds were worthy of note and a shining example to others.

The outstandingly high level of achievement by so many luminaries from the Scots-Irish diaspora in Tennessee, Virginia, Pennsylvania, Kentucky,

North Carolina, Georgia, South Carolina and Texas has to be measured against the great suffering and pain first families endured during early formative years on the frontier.

Faith and Freedom were cherished watchwords of the Scots-Irish Presbyterians, and they maintained these ideals as they moved during the 17th century Plantation years over the short sea journey from Scotland to Ulster, and then trekked arduously across the Atlantic in wooden ships on the adventure into the great unknown of the frontier lands of the 'New World'.

God-fearing Scots-Irish, or Ulster-Scots, combined in their ideals: a total reverence for the Almighty, a deep devotion to their families, sincere love of country and passionate belief in their liberty. Generally as a people the Scots-Irish stayed true to the four main cornerstones of life: God, Country, Family and Liberty, although there were some, as in every community, who did not attain these standards.

The Scots-Irish were well-prepared for establishing settlements on the American frontier. They had endured, for more than a century, life in the harsh, rugged and, in parts, hostile countryside of the north of Ireland and by the time they reached America had survived wars, sieges, famines, drought and religious persecution.

They were a people certainly undeterred by the dangers they faced in their new environment, and most found the wide open spaces to their liking.

Indeed, largely due to past experiences in lowland Scotland and the north of Ireland, Scots-Irish fared much better than other white ethnic groups like the English, Germans, Welsh, Dutch, Scottish Highlanders and Scandinavians in resisting hostilities of the native American tribes; in fending off English, French and Spanish colonial predators and oppressors and in pushing the frontier south and west to its outer limits.

The Scots-Irish effectively set parameters of life in many cities and towns along the western frontier of 18th century America, and with close identification to church, school and home they were able to lay foundations for a civilised society, which placed total emphasis on a belief in God and in the liberty of conscience and democracy.

Celebrated Northern Ireland historian-folklorist the Rev W. F. Marshall summed up their work ethic and commitment to a cause: "The Scots-Irish were the first to start and the last to quit. The vigour and grit of the race were seen in their pioneering instinct."

The early Scots-Irish settlers were willing, even eager, to go beyond the "outer fringe of civilisation" and establish settlements on the frontier. Their experience as colonists in Ireland had made them adaptable and assimilative of the best traits needed for survival on the frontier and their farming methods - the slash-and-burn clearing of farms, corn-based cropping and the running of livestock in open woods - were techniques ideally suited for the southern Appalachian backcountry.

Three hundred years have elapsed since the first Scots-Irish immigrants landed on American soil and, in that time the enormous landscape they inhabited has changed beyond all recognition.

The population has multiplied one hundred times to more than 300 million, with the political, social and cultural perspectives increasingly diverse in what is now an enormous melting pot of humanity.

The fundamentals of Faith and Freedom, so profound, meaningful and enriching to the proud pioneering people from Ulster and lowland Scotland, were permanently enshrined in the constitutional imperatives of the American nation, and today they are testimony to all that was achieved in early formative years of struggle and supreme sacrifice on the frontier.

The Declaration of Independence of July 4, 1776, which at least six Ulstermen helped draw up, contained fine Christian sentiments: "We hold these truths to be self-evident, that men are created equal, that they are endowed by their creator, with certain inalienable rights, that among them are life, liberty, pursuit of happiness."

John Patterson MacLean, noted 19th century historian, said of the Scots-Irish: "They practiced strict discipline in morals and gave instruction to the youth in their schools and in teaching Biblical scriptures. To all this combined in a remarkable degree, acuteness of intellect, firmness of purpose and conscientiousness to duty."

From Pennsylvania through the Shenandoah Valley of Virginia to the Carolinas along the Great Wagon Road they came; to Tennessee, Georgia, Kentucky, on to the territories of Mississippi, Louisiana, Texas, Oklahoma, Kansas, Colorado and California.

The Scots-Irish blazed the pioneering trail in America for others to follow. They were a durable, determined people with the special personal stamp needed to tame the wilds of the frontier, and make it a place for civilised family life.

The Scots-Irish who settled on the American frontier through the 18th century were of the people who moved across from lowland Scotland from 1610 in the Ulster Plantation. They made the short sea journey from Ayrshire, Argyllshire, Renfrewshire, Lanarkshire, Dunfrieshire to principally counties Antrim, Down, Londonderry, Tyrone, Donegal.

In the passage of time, many of them, because of religious persecution and economic deprivation, faced the long arduous trek across the Atlantic.

North Carolina academic James G. Leyburn, in a social history of the Scotch-Irish, described the Scots who moved to Ulster as humble folk with ambition and qualities of character that made good pioneers.

"Even Presbyterian ministers who worked among them in Ulster were usually from humbler walks of Scottish life, for The Kirk offered no sinecures for younger sons of the gentry," said Leyburn

The Scots-Irish were a unique people and the extent of their influence in the establishment of the USA after the Revolutionary War was considerable. Scots-Irish are described as clannish, contentious, hard to get on with, set in their ways.

A Scots-Irish prayer ran: "Lord grant that I may always be right, for Thou knowest I am hard to turn."

·〜39〜·

THE OTHER SCOTS-IRISH
PRESIDENTS

Andrew Jackson was the first American President to have Scots-Irish (Ulster) family roots. Sixteen other United States Presidents have family links to this diaspora.

JAMES KNOX POLK: (Democrat 1845-49). The 11th American President, James Knox Polk was born in 1795 near Charlotte in North Carolina. His Scottish-born great-grandfather Robert Bruce Polk (Pollok), of Lifford (East Donegal), arrived in the American colonies about 1680, settling in Maryland with descendants moving on North Carolina.

James Knox Polk was Governor of Tennessee before becoming President and he and his wife Sarah are buried in Nashville. Both were Presbyterians. Polk served seven terms in the United States Congress and was Speaker of the House, the only President ever to hold this office.

A great uncle Thomas Polk signed, with other Scots-Irish citizens in North Carolina, the Mecklenburg Declaration of May, 1775, a very significant document which preceded the Declaration of Independence of July 4, 1776.

JAMES BUCHANAN: (Democrat 1857-61). Born 1791 at Stone Batter in Cove Gap, Franklin County in Pennsylvania and lived for most of his early life at Mercersburg, Pennsylvania, James Buchanan, the 15th President, was a Presbyterian like his Presidential predecessors Jackson and Polk.

The Buchanan family originated from Deroran near Omagh, Co. Tyrone and his mother and father James and Elizabath Speer Buchanan - left Donegal for America in 1783.

James Buchanan was the only bachelor President. He once declared: "My Ulster blood is my most priceless heritage".

ANDREW JOHNSON: (Democrat 1865-69). Born 1808 in Raleigh, North Carolina, Andrew Johnson's Presbyterian namesake and grandfather from Mounthill outside Larne in Co. Antrim came to America about 1750.

Johnson rose to the Presidency from log cabin origins - his community in North Carolina were known as "the poor Protestants" - and he worked as a tailor for many years after moving to Greeneville in East Tennessee.

He became Mayor of Greeneville, Governor of Tennessee and Vice-President to Abraham Lincoln before assuming the Presidency on Lincoln's assassination. Andrew's wife Eliza McArdle was also of Scots-Irish stock.

ULYSSES SIMPSON GRANT: (Republican 1869-77). Born 1822 in Point Pleasant, Ohio, Grant, also of Presbyterian stock, successfully commanded the Union Army in the America Civil War of 1861-65.

His mother Hannah Simpson was descended from the Simpson family of Dergenagh near Dungannon, Co. Tyrone. His great-grandfather, John Simpson, left Ulster for America in 1760.

President Grant was a Methodist and in 1878 he visited Ulster after his Presidency, receiving the freedom of Londonderry. On that visit, after arriving in Dublin, he travelled by train to Londonderry via Omagh and Strabane,.

He stopped for a time at Ballygawley, Co. Tyrone to see the Grant family homestead. He also visited Coleraine, Co. Londonderry.

CHESTER ALAN ARTHUR: (Republican 1881-85). The 21st American President was born at Fairfield, Vermont in 1830. Arthur's grandfather and his father, Baptist pastor the Rev William Arthur, emigrated to Dunham, Quebec, Canada from Dreen near Cullybackey, Co. Antrim in 1801, and the family settled in the neighbouring American state of Vermont.

Arthur, a graduate of Princeton College and a lawyer who later became a teacher, was an officer in the New York state militia during the Civil War. He was Vice-President for six months to President James A. Garfield, becoming President on Garfield's assassination in September, 1881.

Although of Presbyterian and Baptist family roots, Arthur became an Episcopalian.

GROVER CLEVELAND: (Democrat 1885-89 and 1893-97). The 22nd and 24th President was born 1837 in Caldwell, New Jersey. His maternal grandfather Abner Neal left Co. Antrim in the late 18th century.

Grover was the son of a Presbyterian minister the Rev Richard Falley Cleveland, who ministered in Connecticut, New York and New Jersey. His mother Ann Neal Cleveland was the daughter of a Baltimore book publisher. Grover Cleveland, a lawyer, was Mayor of Buffalo, New York and Governor of New York before rising to the Presidency.

He served two terms in the White House, winning the first and third elections (1884 and 1892) and losing the second (1888) to Benjamin Harrison. Cleveland, a man who weighed 250lbs, retained a deep faith in God and always upheld his strict religious upbringing in a Presbyterian manse.

BENJAMIN HARRISON: (Republican 1889-93). The 23rd American President was born in 1833 at North Bend, Ohio. Harrison, grandson of the ninth President William Henry Harrison, was related to Ulster immigrants James Irwin and William McDowell.

His mother Elizabeth Irwin Harrison was born and raised in Mercersburg, Pennsylvania, a strong Scots-Irish settlement, and his father was a member of the US House of Representatives.

President Harrison was a devout Presbyterian and he chartered a career as a lawyer and brigadier-general soldier in the Civil War. Harrison served in the US Senate for six years (1881-87).

Although he narrowly lost the popular vote in the 1888 Presidential election, he reached the White House by having a sizeable majority of the electoral vote.

WILLIAM McKINLEY: (Republican 1897-1901), Born 1843 in Niles, Ohio. A Presbyterian, he was great grandson of James McKinley, who emigrated to America from Conagher near Ballymoney, Co. Antrim about 1743.

The Presbyterian McKinleys were originally from Perthshire, Scotland and they moved to Ulster in the 17th century Plantation years. McKinley's grandparents fought in the Revolutionary War and the family was involved in iron manufacturing. William McKinley, the 25th United States President, was a US Representative for 12 years and Governor of Ohio for four.

McKinley was assassinated at Buffalo, New York on September 6, 1901. President McKinley married his wife Ida Saxton in a Presbyterian church, but he was a Methodist. He was intensely proud that the Scots-Irish were the first to proclaim for liberty in the United States.

THEODORE ROOSEVELT: (Republican 1905-09). Born 1858 in New York City. 26th President Roosevelt, who wrote admiringly of the courage and exploits of the Scots-Irish on the American frontier, is claimed to have Presbyterian ancestors on his maternal side from Larne, Co. Antrim.

Folklore in East Antrim link him to the Irvines of Carneac near Larne and the Bullochs from the same area. Roosevelt, a distinguished US cavalry officer in the Spanish-American War and New York Governor and politician before becoming President in 1904, belonged to the Dutch Reformed Church.

Roosevelte described the Scots-Irish as "a stern, virile, bold and hardy people who formed the kernel of that American stock who were the pioneers of our people in the march westwards".

WOODROW WILSON (Democrat 1913-21). Born 1856 in Staunton, Virginia. He was the grandson of James Wilson, who emigrated to North Carolina from Dergelt near Strabane, Co. Tyrone.

His father, the Rev Joseph Ruggles Wilson was a Presbyterian minister and Woodrow was a lecturer at Princeton College in New Jersey before becoming President. He visited Ireland in 1899.

Wilson once described his nature as a struggle between his Irish blood - "quick, generous, impulsive, passionate, always anxious to help and to sympathise with those in distress" and his Scottish blood - "canny, tenacious and perhaps a little exclusive".

He also said: "I myself am happy that there runs in my veins a very considerable strain of Irish blood",

HARRY TRUMAN: (Democrat 1949-53). The 33rd President was born 1884 at Lamar, Missouri. His maternal grandfather, Solomon Young was of Scots-Irish settler stock and moved from Kentucky to Kansas City, Missouri in 1840.

President Truman, who also had English and German ancestry, was a popular straight-talking American President after the Second World War. He had been a United States Senator for 10 years from 1935.

Truman was a Baptist, but attended the Presbyterian church as a youth.

RICHARD MILLHOUSE NIXON: (Republican 1969-74). The 37th President was born in 1913 at Yorba Linda, California and had Ulster connections on two sides of his family.

His Nixon Presbyterian ancestors left Co. Antrim for America around 1753, while the Millhouses came from Carrickfergus and Ballymoney, also in Co. Antrim. Richard Nixon, himself, was a Quaker and his wife Thelma Catherine "Pat" Ryan had Irish Roman Catholic family connections.

Nixon, a lawyer and controversial President, served as Vice-President during the two Presidential terms of Dwight D. Eisenhower.

JAMES EARL CARTER: (Democrat 1977-81). The 39th President was born 1924 in Plains, Georgia. Scots-Irish settler Andrew Cowan, believed to come from Co. Antrim, was President Carter's direct descendant on his mother's side.

Cowan, a Presbyterian, was in 1772 one of the first residents of Boonesborough, a frontier buffer zone in the South Carolina Piedmont region. Jimmy Carter, who also has English ancestry, is a Baptist and, since ending his Presidential term, he has been noted for his humanitarian work.

GEORGE BUSH: (Republican 1989-93). The 41st President was born 1924 at Milton, Massachusetts. The Bush family come mainly of English stock, but an ancestor on George Bush's mother's side was William Gault, who was born in Ulster (very probably Co. Antrim!) and with his wife Margaret were first settlers of Tennessee, living in Blount County in 1796, the year Tennessee became a state.

The Gaults were identified by the Bush family as being first families of Tennessee in the research carried out by the East Tennessee Historical Society in Knoxville. George Bush is an Episcopalian.

WILLIAM JEFFERSON CLINTON: (Democrat - 1993-2001). Born 1946 in Hope, Hempstead County, Arkansas. 42nd President Bill Clinton claims to be a relative of Lucas Cassidy, who left Co. Fermanagh for America around 1750.

Lucas Cassidy was of Presbyterian stock, President Clinton is a Baptist. During his eight-year period as President, Bill Clinton made three visits to Northern Ireland to publicly express his full support for the peace process in the Province.

GEORGE W. Bush: (Republican 2001-08). Born 1946 in Texas. President Bush, son of President George Walker Bush, is descended on his father's maternal side from the late 18th century East Tennessee settler William Gault, who was born in the north of Ireland (Co. Antrim).

Like Bill Clinton, President George W. Bush has expressed a strong interest in the affairs of Northern Ireland and visited the Province during his Presidency.

VICE-PRESIDENT:

JOHN C. CALHOUN (Democrat 1825-32 Democrat). Son of a Co. Donegal Presbyterian father Patrick Calhoun and mother Margaret Caldwell, who was Virginia-born of Co. Antrim immigrant parents, this South Carolina statesman was Vice-President to President John Quincy Adams and President Andrew Jackson.

Calhoun, a Covenanting Presbyterian, was the leading South Carolina politician of the early 19th century and was Secretary of State for War under President James Monroe.

Two other American Presidents can claim Irish lineage: JOHN FITZGERALD KENNEDY, whose paternal great-grandfather came from Dunganstown, Co. Wexford and maternal grandfather was also Irish, and RONALD REAGAN, whose paternal line can be traced back to Ballyporeen, Co. Tipperary.

Both were of Irish Roman Catholic stock, but on his mother's side President Reagan had Presbyterian ancestry and he himself was a Presbyterian.

40

Scots-Irish Signers of the American Declaration of Independence

The 56 men from the 13 colonies who signed the American Declaration of Independence in July, 1776 were almost entirely of British family origin. Thirty eight are firmly established of being of English extraction, eight Irish (including six Ulster-Scots), five Welsh, four pure Scottish and one Swedish.

Those with Ulster links were John Hancock, Thomas McKean, George Taylor, James Smith, Matthew Thornton and Edward Rutledge, with Thomas Lynch Jun and George Read from family ties to the south of Ireland. William Whipple, Robert Paine and Thomas Nelson are also believed to have links with the north of Ireland.

Of the 56 signatories of the Declaration, 24 were lawyers and jurists, 11 were merchants, nine farmers and the rest large plantation owners, men of means and well-educated.

Thomas McKean was the son of a Co. Antrim emigrant who settled in Pennsylvania; George Taylor moved to America from Ulster as a 20-year-old in the 1730s; James Smith was born the north of Ireland about 1719 and he arrived in Pennsylvania as a 10-year-old with his Presbyterian family;

Matthew Thornton came to America with his family from Londonderry as a four-year-old in 1718 and they settled in New Hampshire; Edward Rutledge's father Dr John Rutledge from Co. Tyrone emigrated to America in 1735, with the family settling in South Carolina.

Maghera, Co. Londonderry-born Charles Thomson, secretary to the American Continental Congress for 15 years from 1774 to 1789 and a close aide to George Washington, also signed the Declaration, but strictly on account of the office he held.

Thomson, a former university professor at Princeton College, New Jersey, also designed the first Great Seal of America.

American pioneer printer John Dunlap, who printed the first copies of the Declaration of Independence in 1776, was born in Strabane, Co. Tyrone and lived with his uncle William, also a printer, in Philadelphia after his emigration as a young man.

Dunlap was printer to the American Continental Congress throughout the Revolutionary War and, in 1777, he founded the Philadelphia Packet newspaper, which he published daily after 1783. He was a close associate of Charles Thomson, the Ulster-born secretary of the Continental Congress.

As a soldier, John Dunlap served in the first troop of the Philadelphia cavalry, which acted as a bodyguard to General George Washington at the battles of Trenton and Princeton. He was a very generous man and personally contributed 20,000 dollars to supply the US army with provisions and clothing in 1782 during a crucial period in the War. He died in 1812.

Patriot merchant and militia soldier Colonel John Nixon gave the first public reading of the Declaration in Philadelphia on July 8, 1776. Nixon's grandparents were Ulster folk.

·⚶41⚶·

ANOTHER ULSTER JACKSON
OF ACCLAIM IN AMERICA

President Andrew Jackson is arguably the best-known Scots-Irish lumi-
nary in the history of the United States of America, but there was another
Jackson whose gallantry in the field of battle gave him an honoured place
in the annals.

General Thomas Jonathan "Stonewall" Jackson figures high in the list of
Scots-Irish heroes whose outstanding courage and military prowess put him
high on a pedestal, especially in his native Shenandoah Valley of Virginia.

"Stonewall" Jackson may have fought and died on the losing Confederate
side during the Civil War of 1861-65, but he was a soldier of special quality
and his upright Christian ideals marked him down as a true leader of men.

Jackson was given the nickname "Stonewall" at the battle of Bull Run in
Virginia in July 1861 after it was said of him: "This is Jackson, standing a
stone wall". The highly significant role that he played for the Confederates
in this decisive battle earned him promotion to major general.

The Civil War hero was the great grandson of an Ulsterman John Jackson,
who, at the age of 33, emigrated to America in 1748 as "a respectable and
prosperous tradesman", settling in Maryland, and then putting down his
roots in the Shenandoah Valley after passing through West Virginia.

John Jackson's family were lowland Presbyterian Scots who settled in the north of Ireland during the 17th century Scottish Plantation years and defended Londonderry during the Siege of 1688-89.

The Jacksons were scattered across Ulster, some located in the north-west of the province around Londonderry and Coleraine, while others lived in counties Armagh, Down, and Antrim.

Varying claims are made about exactly where in Ulster John Jackson was born. In the biography of "Stonewall" Jackson by English writer Colonel G. F. R Henderson, a letter is referred to which states that the ancestors of the great Confederate general had lived in the parish of Londonderry.

The latter, according to Henderson, was in the possession of Thomas Jackson Arnold, of Beverly, West Virginia, a nephew of General Jackson. Another report, of American origin, gives John Jackson's birthplace as near Coleraine in Co. Londonderry.

Residents, however, in the Birches-Tartaraghan area of Co. Armagh close to the shores of Lough Neagh in the centre of Ulster are adamant that John Jackson was one of their kin. Their belief is reinforced by a plaque unveiled on July 22, 1968 in Ballinary, a section of the Birches, which states that this was the reputed birthplace of John Jackson, great grandfather of Thomas Jonathan "Stonewall" Jackson (1824-1863). The then United States Consul General in Northern Ireland unveiled the plaque at the Ballinary site, located about 70 miles from Londonderry-Coleraine.

Today, there are reportedly more Jacksons living in this part of Co. Armagh than in any other region of Northern Ireland and they are convinced of the local connection with "Stonewall" Jackson's family. John Jackson is traced by the Co. Armagh Jacksons as a grandson of Robert Jackson, and a son of John Jackson, who is buried in Tartaraghan Parish Churchyard.

Another John Jackson, from this area, fought with King William 111 at the Battle of the Boyne in 1690 and his sword and cutlass used in the battle have been displayed at Carrickfergus Castle in Co. Antrim

The Jacksons of Co. Armagh have always been strong supporters of the Orange-Protestant cause in Ireland and today that tradition is manifested in their membership of various Orange lodges in a region, where the Orange Order was founded in 1795. These Jacksons primarily belong to the Church of Ireland (Episcopal) and if the American link is authentic, it would have meant that the emigrant John Jackson and his family almost certainly converted to Presbyterianism when they reached America.

John Jackson had a brief sojourn in London before he reached Maryland in 1748. It was there that he met the girl he was to marry, Elizabeth Cummins, the daughter of a London hotelier, who, when her father died and her mother remarried, decided to emigrate. Elizabeth was a highly educated woman of a large stature, and it was said she was "as remarkable for her strength of intellect as for beauty and physical vigour". John Jackson was a "spare diminutive man, of quiet but determined character, sound judgment and excellent morals."

The pair married in 1755 and within two years they headed to the Shenandoah Valley of Virginia with the great flow of Scots-Irish families, who had moved from Ulster. They settled at Moorefield in Hardy County, West Virginia, but after the French-Indian war of 1754-63, they moved 150 miles westwards to find a home at Buckhannon in Randolph County, Virginia.

In his exploits as an Indian fighter and scout John Jackson amassed sizeable land holdings in the Shenandoah Valley and these he distributed to his eight children. The Jacksons in time became one of the leading families in the Valley. In terms of wealth and influence, Jackson was a Randolph County justice and, in 1779, at the age of 74, he served as a captain of a frontier militia regiment.

Elizabeth Jackson, who had possession of 3,000 acres of land in her own right at Buckhannon, survived her husband and she lived until she was 105. She also showed tenacity and courage in fending of Indian attacks on their home and family records show that even in the most dangerous situations, she never wilted.

Two sons rose to high office. Edward (1759-1828), grandfather of "Stonewall", was Randolph County surveyor, militia colonel, commissioner of revenue and high sheriff. He represented Lewis County in the Virginia Assembly and was "a citizen who acquired some knowledge of medicine, was an expert millwright, and a farmer of more than usual ability".

George, his older brother, after service as a colonel in the Revolutionary War, completed three terms in the American Congress and was a close associate of General Andrew Jackson, later to become President. George and Andrew Jackson were not related, but they frequently talked about their first generation Ulster connections who had moved to America several decades earlier. George Jackson's son, John George Jackson replaced his father in Congress and, as lawyer, he was an articulate spokesman in Washington for the Shanendoah Valley dwellers.

Jonathan Jackson , father of "Stonewall", studied law at the Clarksburg office of his uncle and, although married to the daughter of a merchant from Parslbury, West Virginia, Julie Beeleith Neale, he was never a man of great wealth. He died when his son Jonathan was only three.

John George Jackson married Mary Payne of Philadelphia, a sister of Dolly Madison, wife of James Madison, the fourth President of the United States. This increased the influence of the Jackson clan to the highest level and John George was appointed by Madison's successor in the White House James Monroe, as the first federal judge for the western part of Virginia. A brother, Edward Burke Jackson, was the army surgeon during the Creek Indian War of 1812, a Clarksburg doctor and a member of the American Congress for four years.

It was from this noble family tradition of soldiering and public service that Thomas Jonathan "Stonewall" Jackson emerged and in 1842, at the age of 18, he was given a Congressional appointment to the top American military academy at West Point.

With his father leaving little property on his death and his mother forced to seek the help of her relatives, and the Free Masons to rear the family, before she died four years later, it was a rough upbringing for Thomas Jonathan and his brother Warren and sister Laura. When orphaned they went to live with their father's half-brother on a western Virginia farm.

"Stonewall" was a youth of "exemplary habits, of indomitable will and undoubted courage" and in the rough and tumble of frontier society he demonstrated an integrity and a determination to succeed in life.

Before he enrolled at West Point, "Stonewall" was a constable in his Virginia county executing court decrees, serving warrants, summoning witnesses and collecting debts. The West Point training was far removed from the law-enforcement duties of his frontier homeland, but "Stonewall" adapted well and in 1846 he graduated 17th in a class of 70 which contained men who were to serve as the leading generals in the Civil War, in both the Union and Confederate armies.

"Stonewall" was first assigned as a lieutenant in the Mexican War. Under General Zachary Taylor, a fellow Virginian who later became American President in 1849. He also fought in the Seminole Indian War in Florida and was elevated to major. However, Jackson moved away from the front line of battle in 1851 when he accepted a teaching position at the Virginia Military Institute in Lexington and, although still technically in soldiering, this brought him back into civilian life. The 10 years in Lexington was perhaps the most crucial period of his life and there he was to build a solid base for the later affray at the head of the Virginia Confederate troops in the Civil War.

Thomas Jonathan, although born into a Presbyterian family, had very little religious grounding as a youth and during his early military career. This changed when he met Colonel Francis Taylor, a commandant of his regiment in Mexico and a committed Christian. "Stonewall" studied the Bible for himself and curiosity about various religions even led him to the Roman Catholic archbishop of Mexico for advice. But he was not convinced of the validity of Roman Catholic doctrine and in 1849 he was baptised at the age of 25 into the Episcopal Church, the American branch of Anglicanism.

In Lexington, however, it was the Presbyterian Church - the creed of the pioneering Ulster settlers, which provided him with a spiritual satisfaction and he made his profession of faith as a dissenting Calvinist in November 1851. Soon after he became a Presbyterian elder, and a lay preacher with intent to win souls for Christ.

"Stonewall" married Eleanor Junkin, daughter of the Rev George Junkin, president of Washington College in Virginia, in 1854, but she died 14 months into the marriage. His second marriage in 1857 was to Mary Anna Morrison, daughter of the Rev Dr R. H Morrison, president of Davidson College in North Carolina. They had one daughter.

Religion was the main pre-occupation for "Stonewall" in those Lexington years, and he daily took the Bible as his guide, literally interpreting every word on its pages. He was strict Sabbatarian - never reading on that day, nor posting a letter; he believed that the US federal government in carrying the mail on Sundays was violating a divine law.

To the church, Jackson gave one-tenth of his income, established a Sunday school from his own means and was particularly compassionate about the plight of the black slave children in the area. Jackson's faith transcended every action of his life. He started the day with a blessing and always ended it with thanks to God. His watchword was: "I have long cultivated the most trivial and customary acts of life with a silent prayer."

His two wives, during their marriages, were of similar fundamental Christian outlook, both daughters of the Presbyterian manse. Eleanor Junkin's father was of Scottish Covenanting stock, who had come from Ulster in the late 18th century. The Morrisons were also of Scots-Irish extraction.

Jackson was not a wealthy man, notwithstanding his senior position at Lexington Military College. He depended solely on his salary and both his wives were also of limited means. But he still managed to extend traditional Virginian hospitality to all who came in contact with him.

When the Civil War broke out in April 1861 and Virginia was seceded from the Union , "Stonewall" Jackson answered the Confederate call to action and was commissioned a colonel. He led a detachment of Virginia Military Institute cadets from Lexington to Richmond to defend the Confederate flank there. This led to the command of the Virginia forces at Harper's Ferry, a posting that placed him in the front line.

Jackson distinguished himself at the Battle of Bull Run at Manassas in July 1861, when he inflicted a crushing defeat on the Union Army. The bravery was such that General Bernard E. Bee, commander of the South Carolina Confederacy, cried out to his men to look to Jackson, stating: "There he stands like a stone wall. Rally behind the Virginians". Bee, Jackson's classmate from West Point, died in the battle, but the "Stonewall" tribute became a legend.

At the second Battle of Bull Run in August 1862, "Stonewall" further distinguished himself by his valour. After marching 51 miles in two days, his "foot cavalry" smashed the Union depot at Manassas, went underground for another two days, and then held off superior forces until Confederate re-inforcements could be called. He also had notable battle success at Harper's Valley, Antietam-Sharpsbury and Frederickburg.

"Stonewall" Jackson sadly had his last stand at the Battle of Chancellorsville on May 2, 1863 and the outstanding contribution he and his men made there ensured victory for General Robert E. Lee. However, the advantage from the victory was not to last as the tide gradually turned against the Confederates, due to lack of money and resources.

After his heroics at Bull Run, Jackson, was upgraded to Major-General and placed in charge of the Confederate Army in the lower Shenandoah Valley. His soldiers referred to him as "Old Jack" and his tall, thin frame and long beard belied his barely 40 years. He remained a man of puritan tastes, a non-smoker, non-drinker and non-gambler and he ate sparingly. His commitment to the Confederate cause was total and in uniform he was a stern disciplinarian, but he looked on war as "the sum of all evil".

Jackson moved to attack the Union forces in the Valley and, while they had reversals, they managed to hold the line and send the enemy retreating back to Washington. It was at Chancellorsville that Jackson was a victim of mistaken fire by one of his own men. He lost an arm after being struck three times and had to retire from the battle-field. Death followed quickly when he contacted pneumonia, but in a final order, Jackson called out: "pass the infantry to the front".

His last words underlined his abiding Christian faith: "Let us cross over the river and rest under the shade of the trees". Thomas Jonathan "Stonewall" Jackson was only 39 when he died on May 10, 1863. General Robert E. Lee, who had lost his finest soldier, said: "I know not how to replace him". Jackson was much respected even by enemy officers on the Union side for his heroism, bravery, devotion to duty and purity of character.

He was the true Christian patriot and President Abraham Lincoln, who died within two years, described him as "a very brave soldier".

Jackson's death two years into the Civil War had fuelled debate as to what might have happened if he had lived. Serious reversals in the Shenandoah Valley and at Gettysburg sealed the fate of the Confederacy, for without the sterling leadership qualities of the redoubtable "Stonewall", the Johnny Rebs were never the same potent force again. Economic factors also negated their war effort.

The heroics in battle of the gallant "Stonewall" Jackson were in the best Scots-Irish tradition. He was a soldier of a very special quality.

THOMAS JONATHAN
"STONEWALL" JACKSON

THEODORE ROOSEVELT AS A COLONEL

·❧42❧·

A Celebrated American's
View of the Scots-Irish

President Theodore Roosevelt, in his best-selling book 'The Winning of the West', gave a very illuminating and accurate description of the Scots-Irish who pioneered the American frontier in the 18th century.

Roosevelt, part of whose family roots can be traced back to Co. Antrim, fully understood and was a keen admirer of the sterling qualities of the people who tamed the outer American frontier in the 18th century.

His celebrated and fulsome tribute to this "stern and virile" people has been widely documented:

"Along the western frontier of the colonies that were so soon to be the United States, among the foothills of the Alleghenies, on the slopes of the wooded mountains, and in the long trough-like valleys that lay between the ranges, dwelt a peculiar and characteristically American people.

"These frontier folk, the people of the up-country, or back-country, who lived near and among the forest-clad mountains, far away from the long-settled districts of flat coastal plan and sluggish tidal river, were known to themselves and to others as backwoodsmen.

"They all bore a strong likeness to one another in their habits of thought and ways of living, and differed markedly from the people of the older and more civilised communities to the eastward.

"The western border of the country was then formed by the great-barrier chains of the Alleghenies, which ran north and south from Pennsylvania, through Maryland, Virginia and Carolina, the trend of the valleys being parallel to the sea-coast and the mountains rising highest to the southward.

"It was difficult to cross the ranges from east to west, but it was both easy and natural to follow the valleys between. From Fort Pitt to the high hill-homes of the Cherokees this great tract of wooded and mountainous country possessed nearly the same features and characteristics, differing utterly in physical aspect from the alluvial plains bordering the ocean.

"So likewise, the backwoods mountaineers who dwelt near the great watershed that separates the Atlantic stream, from the springs of the Watauga, the Kanawha and the Monongahela were all cast in the same mould and resembled much more than any of them did their immediate neighbors of the plains.

"The backwoodsmen of Pennsylvania had little in common with the peaceful population of Quakers and Germans who lived between the Delaware and the Susquehanna and their near kinsmen of the Blue Ridge and the Great Smoky Mountains were separated by an equally wide gulf from the aristocratic planter communities that flourished in the tide-water regions of Virginia and the Carolinas.

Near the coast the lines of division between the colonies corresponded fairly well with the differences between the populations; but after striking the foothills, though the political boundaries continued to go east and west, those both of ethnic and of physical significance began to run north and south.

"The backwoodsmen were Americans by birth and parentage, and of mixed race; but the dominant strain in their blood was that of Presbyterian Irish - the Scotch-Irish, as they were often called.

"Full credit had been awarded the Roundhead and the Cavalier for their leadership in our history; nor have we been altogether blind to the deeds of the Hollander and the Huguenot, but it is doubtful if we have fully realised the importance of the part played by that stern and virile people, the Irish whose preachers taught the creed of Knox and Calvin.

"These Irish representatives of the Covenanters were in the west almost what the Puritans were in the north-east and more than the Cavaliers were in the south. Mingled with descendants of many other races, they nevertheless formed the kernel of the distinctively and intensely American stock who were the pioneers of our people in their march westwards, the vanguard of the army of fighting settlers, who with axe and rifle won their way from the Alleghenies to the Rio Grande and the Pacific.

"The Presbyterian Irish were themselves already a mixed people. Though mainly descended from Scotch ancestors - who came originally from both lowlands and highlands, from among both the Scotch Saxons and the Scotch Celts - many of them were of English, a few of French Huguenot, and quite a number of the true old Misesian Irish extradition.

"They were the Protestants of the Protestants; they detested the Catholics, whom they had conquered, and regarded the Episcopalians by whom they themselves had been oppressed, with a more sullen, but scarcely less intense hatred.

"They were a truculent and obstinate people, and gloried in the warlike renown of their forefathers, the men who had followed Cromwell, and who had shared in the defence of Derry and in the victories of the Boyne and Aughrim."

"They did not begin to come to America in any numbers till after the opening of the 18th century; by 1730 they were fairly swarming across the ocean, for the most part in two streams, the larger going to the port of Philadelphia, the smaller to Charleston.

"Pushing through the long settled lowlands of the seacoast, they at once made their abode at the foot of the mountains and became the outposts of civilisation. From Pennsylvania, wither the great majority of them had come, they drifted south along the foothills and down the long valleys, till they met their brethren from Charleston, who had pushed up into the Carolina back-country.

"In this land of hills, covered by unbroken forest, they took root and flourished, stretching in a broad belt from north to south, a shield of sinewy men thrust in between the people of the seaboard and the red warriors of the wilderness.

"All through this region they were alike; as they had so little kinship with the Cavalier as with the Quaker; the West was won by those who have been rightly called the Roundheads of the south, the same men, who, before any others declared for American Independence.

"The two facts of most importance to remember in dealing with our pioneer history are, first, that the western portions of Virginia and the Carolinas were people by an entirely different stock from that which had long existed in the Tidewater regions of these colonies, and, secondly, except for those in the Carolinas who came from Charleston, the immigrants of this stock were mostly from the north, from the great breeding ground and nursery in western Pennsylvania.

"That these Irish Presbyterians were a bold and hardy race is proved by their at once pushing past the settled regions, and plunging into the wilderness as the leaders of the white advance. They were the first and last set of immigrants to do this; all others have merely followed in the wake of their predecessors. But indeed, they were fitted to be Americans from the very start.

"They were kinsfolk of the Covenanters; they deemed it a religious duty to interpret their own Bible, and held for a divine right the election of their own clergy. For generations their whole ecclesiastic and scholastic systems had been fundamentally democratic. In the hard life of the frontier they lost much of their religion, and they had but scant opportunity to give their children the schooling in which they believed; but what few meeting-houses and school-houses there were on the borders were theirs.

"The numerous families of colonial English who came among them adopted their religion if they adopted any. The creed of the backwoodsmen who had a creed at all was Presbyterianism; for the Episcopacy of the tide-water lands obtained no foothold in the mountains, and the Methodists and Baptists had just begun to appear in the west when the Revolution broke out."

— THEODORE ROOSEVELT.

BIBLIOLOGY:

THE LIFE AND TIMES OF ANDREW JACKSON by W. W. Brands. Published by Doubleday, New York and London.

HOUSTON AND CROCKETT: HEROES OF TENNESSEE AND TEXAS - AN ANTHOLOGY. Edited by Herbert L. Harper. Published by Tennessee Historical Commission.

AMERICAN LEGEND: THE REAL LIFE ADVENTURES OF DAVID CROCKETT by Buddy Levy. Published by G. P. Putnam's Sons, New York.

ANDREW JACKSON by Sean Wilentz. Published by Times Books, New York.

IN THE FOOTSTEPS OF DAVY CROCKETT by Randell Jones. Published by John F. Blair, Winston Salem, North Carolina.

THE HERMITAGE: HOME OF ANDREW JACKSON. Published by the Ladies' Hermitage Association, Nashville (1997).

LIFE OF ANDREW JACKSON by J. S. Bassett. Published by Doubleday, Page and Co..

JACKSON'S WAY by John Buchanan. Published by John Wilson and Sons Inc., New York.

THE TRUE ANDREW JACKSON by Cyrus Townsend Brady. Published by J. B. Lippincott and Co..

LIFE OF ANDREW JACKSON by James Parton (Volume 1) by Riverside Press, Boston and New York.

HISTORY OF ANDREW JACKSON by Augustus C. Buell. Published by Charles Scribners, New York.

ANDREW JACKSON - THE GENTLE SAVAGE by David Karsner. Published by Brentanos, New York.

THE PASSIONS OF ANDREW JACKSON by Andrew Burstein.

THE COMPLETE BOOK OF UNITED STATES PRESIDENTS by William A. Degregorio. Published by Wings Books, New Jersey.

SAM HOUSTON: AMERICAN GIANT by M. K. Wisehart. Published by Robert B. Luce, Washington.

SAM HOUSTON by James L. Haley. Published by University of Oklahoma Press.

THE RAVEN: THE LIFE STORY OF SAM HOUSTON by Marquis James. Published by The Bobbs-Merrill Company, Indianapolis.

SAM HOUSTON: MAN OF DESTINY by Clifford Hopewell.

SAM HOUSTON: THE LIFE AND TIMES OF THE LIBERATOR OF TEXAS - AN AUTHENTIC AMERICAN HERO by John Hoyt Williams. Published by Promontory Press, New York

SAM HOUSTON AND THE AMERICAN SOUTH-WEST by Randolph Campbell.

SAM HOUSTON: THE TALLEST TEXAN by William Johnson.

AMERICAN NATIONAL BIOGRAPHY by John A. Garraty and Mark C. Carnes.

DAVID CROCKETT (THE MAN BEHIND THE MYTH) by James Wakefield Burke.

UNIVERSITY OF TENNESSEE THESIS: THE PUBLIC CAREER OF DAVID CROCKETT by Anna Grace Caron (August 1955).

DRT LIBRARY at The Alamo, Texas.

DICTIONARY OF AMERICAN BIOGRAPHY (Volume 9).

THE STORY OF THE ALAMO. Published by the Daughters of the Republic of Texas, San Antonio.

DAVY CROCKETT: THE MAN, THE LEGEND, THE LEGACY by Frank Mayo.

LONE STAR: A HISTORY OF TEXAS AND THE TEXANS BY T. R. FEHRENBACH. Published by Tess Press, New York.

CARRICKFERGUS: A STROLL THROUGH TIME by Charles McConnell. Published by Carrickfergus Publications (1994).

PRESBYTERIANS IN IRELAND: AN ILLUSTRATED HISTORY by :Laurence Kirkpatrick. Published by Booklink, Holywood, Co. Down.

DAVID CROCKETT; THE MAN AND THE LEGEND by James Shackford. (Published 1956).

THE CROCKETT CHRONICLE.

DAVID CROCKETT'S OWN STORY (AS WRITTEN BY HIMSELF). Published Citadel press, New York.

CALENDAR (2000) OF EARLY TEXAS AND THE REPUBLIC OF TEXAS HISTORY.

SMITHSONIAN PRESIDENTS by Carter Smith. Barnes and Noble Publishing.

TO THE BEST OF MY ABILITY: THE AMERICAN PRESIDENTS - James M. McPherson (general editor). Published by Dorling Kindersley, New York.

THE BATTLE OF NEW ORLEANS by Robert V. Remini. Published by Penguin Group, New York.

YOUNG HICKORY: THE MAKING OF ANDREW JACKSON by Hendrik Booraem. Published by Taylor Trade Publishing, Texas.

DONEGAL ANNUAL: Journal of the Co. Donegal Historical Society.

THE WINNING OF THE WEST by Theodore Roosevelt.

AN INTERVIEW WITH ANDREW JACKSON by Ruth Smalley. Published by The Overmountain Press, Johnson City, Tennessee.

IN THE FOOTSTEPS OF DAVY CROCKETT by Randell Jones. Published by John F. Blair, Winston Salem, North Carolina.

THREE ROADS TO THE ALAMO by William C. Davis. Published by Harper Publications.

BOLD LEGACY: THE STORY OF THE HOUSTON-HUSTON ANCESTORS (1150 to 1800 by Cleburne Huston).

ANDREW JACKSON AND THE COURSE OF THE BRITISH EMPIRE 1767-1821 by Robert V. Remini. Published by Harper and Row, New York.

MESSAGE AND PAPERS OF THE PRESIDENTS by James D. Richardson.

THE LIFE OF ANDREW JACKSON by Robert V. Remini.

AUTHOR'S ACKNOWLEDGEMENTS:

Dr Samuel Lowry, Ambassador International Publications, Belfast and Greenville, South Carolina.

Tim Lowry, Ambassador International, Greenville, South Carolina.

David Wright (artist), Gallatin, Tennessee.

Cherel Henderson, Director East Tennessee Historical Society, Knoxville.

Sally A. Baker, David Crockett Museum, Morristown, Tennessee.

John Rice Irwin, Museum of Appalachia, Norris, Tennessee.

Joseph J. Swann, Mayor of Maryville, Tennessee, and David Crockett historian.

Staff at Calvin M. McClung Historical and Archives Museum, Knoxville, Tennessee.

George Patton, Chief Executive, Ulster-Scots Agency, Belfast.

Marcia Mullin, Curator, The Hermitage, Nashville, Tennessee.

Larry Crabtree, Huntsville, Alabama.

Dr David Hume, Larne, Co. Antrim.

Glen Pratt, Canyon, Texas.

Sam Wyly, Dallas, Texas.

Councillor Dr Ian Adamson OBE, Belfast.

Marie Fullington, Tourism Ireland, New York.

William Chemerka, Editor, Crockett Chronicle, New Jersey.

Joy N. Bland, Historian of Direct Descendants of David Crockett and Kin, Paris, Tennessee.

Fred Brown, Knoxville News-Sentinel, Tennessee.

Dr George Schweitzer, University of Tennessee and East Tennessee Historical Society, Knoxville.

Wilhelmina Williams, Greeneville, Tennessee.

Belinda Mahaffy, Lifford, Co. Donegal.

Robert Crockett, Coshquin, Londonderry.

Billy Crockett, Upperlands, Co. Londonderry.

Daughters of the Republic of Texas, San Jacinto Chapter, Houston, Texas.

Daughters of the Republic of Texas, San Antonio, Texas.

Edwin Poots MLA, Northern Ireland Minister for Culture, Arts and Leisure.

Marylin Bell Hughes, Tennessee State Library and Archives, Nashville, Tennessee.

Linda Patterson, Ambassador International Publications, Belfast.

Gillian Graham, Ambassador International Publications, Belfast.

Michelle Inafuku, Emerald House International Publications, Greenville, South Carolina.

Christ McIvor, Librarian, Ulster-America Folk Park, Omagh, Co. Tyrone (Centre for Emigration Studies).

Christine Johnston, Library, Ulster-American Folk Park, Omagh, Co. Tyrone (Centre for Emigration Studies).

Roy A. Jack, Newtownstewart, Co. Tyrone.

Stephen Graham, Armagh.

Francis Trimble, Houston, Texas.

Ann Toplovich, Director Tennessee, Historical Society, Nashville.

Kelly Wilkerson, Tennessee Historical Society, Nashville.

Caroll Ostrom, Museum of Appalachia, Norris, Tennessee.

Robert L. Schaadt, Director , Sam Houston Regional Library and Research Center, Liberty, Texas.

David Siglin, A&E Media, Greenville, South Carolina

Robert Anderson, Richhill, Co. Armagh

The author acknowledges the support and sponsorship of Tourism Ireland on his various visits to the United States. Tourism Ireland actively promotes and markets in the United States holidays in both Northern Ireland and in the Republic of Ireland and this has resulted in an increasing number of Americans with family roots in Ireland coming on sight-seeing visits or for genealogical research work.

There are few artists in the United States who have left such an important mark on the art of the American frontier as David Wright, of Gallatin, Tennessee. Known for his exhaustive execution for authentic detail and historical accuracy, Wright has also expanded his role to that of Art Director for epic size productions in historic documentaries and films. Wright's works can be seen at www. davidwrightart.com

PICTURES AND ILLUSTRATIONS:

David Wright, Nashville, Tennessee.

Gray Stone Press, Nashville, Tennessee.

The Hermitage, Nashville, Tennessee.

The Ulster-Scots Agency, Belfast.

Daughters of the Republic of Texas, San Antonio, Texas.

Images of Sam Houston and David Crockett, Tennessee State Library and Archives, Nashville.

Museum of Appalachia, Norris, Knoxville, Tennessee.

Friends of the Governor's Mansion, Austin, Texas.

Larry Crabtree, Huntsville, Alabama.

News Letter, Belfast.

Sally A. Baker, David Crockett Museum, Morristown, Tennessee.

San Jacinto Museum of History, Houston, Texas.

Fall of the Alamo by Robert Jenkins Onderdonk, used by kind permission of the Governor's Mansion, Austin, Texas.

Sam Houston Regional Library and Research Center, Liberty, Texas.

AUTHOR BILLY KENNEDY IS:

1. An Honorary Citizen of Knoxville, Tennessee (granted by Mayor Phil Haslem, March 8, 2008).

2. An Honorary Citizen of Louisville, Kentucky (granted by Mayor Daniel L. Armstrong, March 14, 2002).

3. An Honorary Citizen of Newnan, Georgia

4. He was officially welcomed to the City of Philadelphia, Pennsylvania by Mayor Edward G. Randell (March 14, 1998).

5. He has received a Certificate of Appreciation by the Andrew Jackson Chapter, Nashville, of the National Society of the Sons of the American Revolution (October 17, 2006).

6. He holds honorary membership of the First Families of Tennessee (granted by the East Tennessee Historical Society - May 14, 2003).

7. His work has been acknowledged by President Bill Clinton and wife Hillary (January 10, 1996); by President Jimmy Carter (January 9, 1998); by Philip Lader, United States Ambassador to the United Kingdom (January 21, 1998); by Senator Edward Kennedy (1998); by Joseph A. Swann, Mayor of Maryville, Tennessee (in Proclamation issued March 7, 2008); by the Scotch-Irish Society of the United States of America in Citation (March, 1998) and holds honorary membership of the Society.

INDEX

THE SCOTS-IRISH CHRONICLES

by Billy Kennedy

THE SCOTS-IRISH IN THE HILLS of TENNESSEE

This book centered in Tennessee is the definite story of how the American frontier of the late 18th century was advanced and the indomitable spirit of the Scots-Irish shines though on every page. From the Great Smoky Mountain region to the Cumberland Plateau and the Mississippi delta region, the Scots-Irish created a civilisation out of a wilderness. The inheritance they left was hard-won, but something to cherish. The careers of Tennessean Presidents Andrew Jackson, James Knox Polk and Andrew Johnson and state luminaries Davy Crockett and Sam Houston are catalogued in the book.

THE SCOTS-IRISH IN THE SHENANDOAH VALLEY

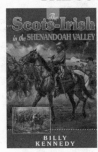

The beautiful Shenandoah Valley alongside the majestic backdrop of the Blue Ridge Mountains of Virginia is the idyllic setting for the intriguing story of a brave resolute people who tamed the frontier. The Ulster-Scots (Scots-Irish) were a breed of people who could move mountains. They did this literally with their bare hands in regions like the Shenandoah Valley, winning the day for freedom and liberty of conscience in the United States. In the Shenandoah Valley, the Scots-Irish led the charge for the American patriots in the Revolutionary War and for the Confederates in the Civil War a century later.

THE SCOTS-IRISH IN THE CAROLINAS

The Piedmont areas of the Carolinas, North and South, were settled by tens of thousands of Scots-Irish Presbyterians in the second half of the 18th century. Some moved down the Great Wagon Road from Pennsylvania, others headed to the up-country after arriving at the port of Charleston. The culture, political heritage and legacy of the Scots-Irish so richly adorned the fabric of American life and the Carolinas was an important homeland for many of these people. It was also the launching pad for the long trek westwards to new lands and the fresh challenge of the expanding frontier.

THE SCOTS-IRISH IN PENNSYLVANIA-KENTUCKY

Pennsylvania and Kentucky are two American states settled primarily at opposite ends of the 18th century by Ulster-Scots Presbyterians, yet this book details how the immigrant trail blended in such diverse regions. William Penn and the Quaker community encouraged the European settlers to move in large numbers to the colonial lands of Pennsylvania from the beginning of the 18th century and the Scots-Irish were the earliest settlers to set up homes in cities like Philadelphia and Pittsburgh. Kentucky, established as a state in 1792, was pioneered by Ulster-Scots families who moved through the Cumberland Gap and down the Wilderness Road with explorer Daniel Boone.

FAITH AND FREEDOM: The SCOTS-IRISH IN AMERICA

A common thread runs through Pennsylvania, Virginia, North Carolina, South Carolina, Tennessee, West Virginia Georgia, Kentucky, Alabama and other neighbouring states - that of a settlement of people who had firmly set their faces on securing for all time - their Faith and Freedom. This inspirational journey of the Scots-Irish Presbyterian settlers details how they moved the American frontier to its outer limits, founding log cabin churches that were to spiral the message of the gospel and establishing schools, which were to expand into some of the foremost educational institutions in the United States.

HEROES OF THE SCOTS-IRISH IN AMERICA

Heroism was a distinct characteristic of the 18th century Scots-Irish immigrants and the raw courage shown by these dogged determined people in very difficult circumstance helped make the United States great. Forging a civilisation out of a wilderness was a real challenge for the Ulster settlers and how well they succeeded in moulding a decent law-abiding society, from the eastern seaboard states, through the Appalachian region into the south to Texas and beyond. The Scots-Irish heroes and heroines have become enshrined in American history, not just as Presidents, statesmen, soldiers and churchmen, but many plain ordinary citizens whose quiet, unselfish deeds were worthy of note, and a shining example to others.

THE MAKING of AMERICA: HOW THE SCOTS-IRISH SHAPED A NATION

In establishing of the United States, the Scots-Irish were one of the most highly influential groups, both in the signing of the American Declaration of Independence on July 4, 1776 and in the Revolutionary War which followed. This group of dedicated stalwarts, whose families emigrated to America from the Irish province of Ulster throughout the 18th century were resolute and uncompromising champions of the movement for American independence. Bitter experience of religious discrimination and economic deprivation in their Scottish and Ulster homelands gave impetus to the Scots-Irish throwing off the shackles of the old order when they moved to the American colonies and opened up the great frontier lands. The Scots-Irish were in the vanguard of American patriot involvement on all fronts of the Revolutionary War , but it was on the frontier that they made their most significant contribution. Quite uniquely as a people they rose to the awesome challenge of the American frontier - its danger, its inaccessibility and its sheer enormity.

WOMEN of the FRONTIER

American frontier women of the 19th century were an extraordinary people whose contribution to the creation of the United States is one of most enduring stories in history. The gallant women of the frontier have never been given the full credit which they deserve for settling, with their families, in an uninhabited wilderness. This book places on record the notable achievements of these heroines. The book gives recognition to the women whose lot was far from glamorous in the bleak and lonely frontier territories. They faced personal hardships and tragedies in hazardous conditions. While the men toiled arduously from dawn to dusk to lay down a stake in the New World, the women were the cornerstone of the home the church and the wider community. Women had to be strong, self-reliant, resourceful and loyal to their families. Through their honest and dedicated endeavours on the frontier, a democratic and decent civilisation emerged which now extends across the great American expanse from the Atlantic to the Pacific. Indeed the women of the American frontier deserve our honour and admiration.

OUR MOST PRICELESS HERITAGE: THE LASTING LEGACY
of the SCOTS-IRISH in AMERICA

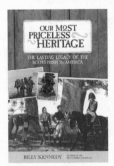

From their earliest arrival in America 350 years ago, the Scots-Irish left lasting legacy, a heritage that was firmly grounded in freedom and democracy.

The pioneering instinct of this proud race from Ulster and Scotland opened up America from the Atlantic coast-line to the Pacific shore - "Sea to Shining Sea" - over a period of several centuries.

The history of the United States is inter-woven with the outstanding personalities from the Scots-Scots diaspora and the distinctive characteristics of a people who pushed the frontier to new horizons.

This competitive study of the Scots-Irish in America by Northern Ireland author Billy Kennedy has created a much greater awareness of the accomplishments and the durability of their hardy settlers and their families who moved to the New World's during the 18th century and created a civilisation out of a wilderness.

It was President James Buchanan, son of a Co. Tyrone man, who said: "My Ulster Blood is My Most Priceless Heritage".

This is a sentiment echoed by many, many people in the United States today!

These books are available from authorised booksellers in the United Kingdom, the United States and the Republic of Ireland or direct from the publishers in Belfast (Northern Ireland) and Greenville (South Carolina).